3+3

Praise for the series:

It was only a matter of time before a clever publisher realized that there is an audience for whom *Exile on Main Street* or *Electric Ladyland* are as significant and worthy of study as *The Catcher in the Rye* or *Middlemarch*. . . . The series . . . is freewheeling and eclectic, ranging from minute rock-geek analysis to idiosyncratic personal celebration —*The New York Times Book Review*

Ideal for the rock geek who thinks liner notes just aren't enough —*Rolling Stone*

One of the coolest publishing imprints on the planet —*Bookslut*

These are for the insane collectors out there who appreciate fantastic design, well-executed thinking, and things that make your house look cool. Each volume in this series takes a seminal album and breaks it down in startling minutiae. We love these. We are huge nerds —*Vice*

A brilliant series . . . each one a work of real love —*NME* (UK)

Passionate, obsessive, and smart —*Nylon*

Religious tracts for the rock 'n' roll faithful —*Boldtype*

[A] consistently excellent series —*Uncut* (UK)

We . . . aren't naive enough to think that we're your only source for reading about music (but if we had our way . . . watch out). For those of you who really like to know everything there is to know about an album, you'd do well to check out Bloomsbury's "33 1/3" series of books —*Pitchfork*

For almost 20 years, the 33-and-a-Third series of music books has focused on individual albums by acts well known (Bob Dylan, Nirvana, Abba, Radiohead),cultish (Neutral Milk Hotel, Throbbing Gristle, Wire) and many levels in-between. The range of music and their creators defines "eclectic", while the writing veers from freewheeling to acutely insightful. In essence, the books are for the music fan who (as Rolling Stone noted) "thinks liner notes just aren't enough." —*The Irish Times*

For reviews of individual titles in the series, please visit our blog at 333sound.com and our website at https://www.bloomsbury.com/academic /music-sound-studies/ Follow us on Twitter: @333books Like us on Facebook: https://www.facebook.com/33.3books

For a complete list of books in this series, see the back of this book.

Forthcoming in the series:

and many more . . .

3+3

Darrell M. McNeill

BLOOMSBURY ACADEMIC
NEW YORK · LONDON · OXFORD · NEW DELHI · SYDNEY

BLOOMSBURY ACADEMIC
Bloomsbury Publishing Inc
1385 Broadway, New York, NY 10018, USA
50 Bedford Square, London, WC1B 3DP, UK
29 Earlsfort Terrace, Dublin 2, Ireland

BLOOMSBURY, BLOOMSBURY ACADEMIC and the Diana logo are trademarks
of Bloomsbury Publishing Plc

First published in the United States of America 2024

Copyright © Darrell M. McNeill, 2024

For legal purposes the Acknowledgments on p. vi constitute an
extension of this copyright page.

Library of Congress Cataloging-in-Publication Data
Names: McNeill, Darrell M., author.
Title: 3+3 / Darrell M. McNeill.
Other titles: Isley Brothers' 3+3 | 3 plus 3
Description: New York: Bloomsbury Academic, 2024. | Series: 33 1/3 |
Includes bibliographical references. | Summary: "Discusses America's most
tenured rock and roll band (of 66 years), their breakout masterpiece album,
3+3, and the twists and turns of being a foundational Black act in rock music
navigating institutional racism in the music business"– Provided by publisher.
Identifiers: LCCN 2023053386 (print) | LCCN 2023053387 (ebook) |
ISBN 9798765106716 (paperback) | ISBN 9798765106723 (epub) |
ISBN 9798765106747 (pdf) | ISBN 9798765106730
Subjects: LCSH: Isley Brothers. | Isley Brothers. 3+3. | African American
rock musicians. | Rock music–United States–1971-1980–History and
criticism. | Music and race–United States–20th century.
Classification: LCC ML421.I84 M36 2024 (print) | LCC ML421.I84 (ebook) |
DDC 782.42166092–dc23/eng/20231208
LC record available at https://lccn.loc.gov/2023053386
LC ebook record available at https://lccn.loc.gov/2023053387

ISBN: PB: 979-8-7651-0671-6
ePDF: 979-8-7651-0674-7
eBook: 979-8-7651-0672-3

Series: 33 $\frac{1}{3}$

Typeset by Deanta Global Publishing Services, Chennai, India
Printed and bound in Great Britain

To find out more about our authors and books visit www.bloomsbury.com
and sign up for our newsletters.

Contents

Acknowledgments

I'm just so glad to be here tonight to talk about my good friends . . . The Isley Brothers. . . . They are great. . . . They've always been good. . . . I'm talkin' 'bout the real thing. . . . They've always been in my heart. I think they're overdue. . . . They were the first rock and roll group that I ever heard in my *life*! Before anybody started usin' the word "rock and roll." . . . Because rock and roll ain't nothin' but rhythm and blues up tempo, that's all rock and roll is. . . ! I don't know why everybody's tryin' to make it somethin' else! They are the founders! They are the originators! They are the creators! They are the emancipators! The architect of what they're doin'! One of the greatest groups in the WORLD! The rock and roll giants! The creators of these groups, they're the ones that STARTED that. . . ![1]
—*Excerpt from Little Richard's 1992 speech inducting The Isley Brothers into the Rock & Roll Hall of Fame*

The Isley Brothers have been an integral part of my ecosystem since I was two years old: my earliest cognitive memories include two pivotal 45s, "It's Alright," by The Impressions, and "This Old Heart of Mine (Is Weak for You)," by The Isley

Brothers—these records were the launchpad to my multi-decade career in music. The inflection point came seven years later, my father holding court in front of the stereo, requisite Cutty and Viceroy in hand. Screaming guitars threatened to tear paint off our walls. On the floor, a black album jacket featuring six glowering brothers in ornate silks, leathers, and denims. My nine-year-old brain reasoned they made those sounds and I wanted to make those sounds, too. *The Isley Brothers: 3+3* embedded in my young psyche like nothing else—not even Hot Wheels, Gigantor, or the Yankees.

The Isleys remain a criminally slighted keystone to any legitimate grasp of Black—therefore, by extension, *American*—pop music. They are one of the last Black rock and roll groups still active since the genre was originally recognized, spending their peak years navigating an environment where rock effectively metamorphosed into a White-exclusive cultural arena. They are among countless Black figures in rock who've been reduced to subordinate status or redacted entirely, never fully receiving recognition nor compensation comparative to their White peers—schisms documented voluminously as being exacerbated by the music industry and target-specific (i.e., segregated) media: a 1987 NAACP Report, "The Discordant Sound Of Music," declared, "No other industry in America so openly classifies its operations on a racial basis. . . . The structure of the industry allows for total White control and domination."

Raised on equal parts urban, AOR, and Top 40 radio in the nation's most cosmopolitan polyglot city—New York, NY—this sophistry of rock and roll being a "Whites Only" tableau was entirely dissonant to me. I knew The Isley Brothers were *definitionally* rock artists, as were Sly & The Family Stone, Band of Gypsys, Labelle, Shuggie Otis, Richie Havens, Rufus, Stevie Wonder, Betty Davis, Funkadelic, and myriad others. And this was *before* my immersion in pioneers like Ike & Tina Turner, Little Richard, Big Mama Thorton, Chuck Berry, The Coasters, Fats Domino, and before them, all the jump blues, boogie-woogie, taproot Blues, gospel, and Black Americana greats who laid rock's foundation. The math on rock fabricated by a huge chunk of its White producers, gatekeepers, and followers was/is anathema to the facts.

This book isn't just a peel-back on the Isleys' creative process for one album but a dissection of the cultural processes that prevented this and their other peak-era albums from reaching critical mass and benefiting from the same support their White peers enjoyed as a matter of course. That 3+3 sold two million units across all formats, in spite of both passive/active-aggressive resistance, is confirmation of oppositional components contributing in equal measure to its brilliance.

I first must humbly acknowledge and thank Leah Babb-Rosenfeld, Sean Maloney, and the entire Bloomsbury team for seeing the value in my proposal and inviting me to contribute to this revered collection of books.

My thanks to my extended family of industry professionals, scholars, and writers who were invaluable in my research: Kevin Goins, Jimi Hazel, Rickey Vincent, Dr. Scot Brown, Nona Hendryx, Eddie Martinez, Maureen Mahon, Shelley Nicole Jefferson, Michael A. Gonzales, Harold Brown (WAR), Steve Ivory, Greg Williams (Switch), Bob Davis, Miles Marshall Lewis, LaFrae Sci, Honeychild Coleman,

Kelsey Warren, Leah King, LaRonda Davis, and my brothers Earl Douglas and Vernon Reid.

I am eternally grateful to my Black Rock Coalition family for giving me the clarity of mission, the soundness of counsel, and the strength of platform to advance this work. I am blessed to be surrounded by such an amazing community.

Love to my entire LaGuardia High School of Music and Art family (Class of 1981, especially). Thanks for painting a picture of a world worth aspiring to, fighting for, and dedicating myself to bringing to fruition.

Peace to my family in the Creative Unity Collective, with extra dap to my brothers Michael Mabern, Yusuf Lamont, and Rodney Black.

Shout out to *The Village Voice* for giving me my bearings as a writer, specifically my mentors Richard Goldstein, Thulani Davis, and Joe Conason. Hugs to Scott Poulson-Bryant, Amy Linden, Miles Marshall Lewis, Michael "Gonzo" Gonzales, and Harry Allen. Rest in power: Nat Hentoff, Stanley Crouch, Jack Newfield, Greg Tate, and The GREAT Wayne Barrett. Thanks to all the media platforms that gave me a chance to shine: VIBE, BRE, WBAI, Bob Davis (Soul-Patrol .com), WPS1/Clocktower, Kandia Crazy Horse (Palgrave Publishing), and CCA Wattis Institute for Contemporary Arts/Sternberg Press.

Gratitude to my Brooklyn Academy of Music (BAM) family. I especially thank my mentor, Joe Melillo—I am forever indebted to you, Joe.

Respect to all the mentors, colleagues, and friends who have lifted me up: James R. Murphy, Chuck Sutton (RIP), Mark Warren (RIP), Jeannie Hopper, Bill "Rosko" Mercer

(RIP), Bruce Mack, Jimmy Saal, Bill Bragin, Nona Hendryx, Garland Jeffreys, Danny Simmons, Kris J. Kraus, Harold Brown, Dr. Ricardo Wilson, Bob Davis, Limor Tomer, Delphine Blue, Jordyn Thiessen, Anthony J. Sloan, Brian Tate, Bill Toles, Al "Rhino" Pereira, Anastas Hackett, Peter Roze, Sidney Howell (RIP), Rose Brackeen, Rod Shepard, and others. Rest in reverence: Tom Terrell, Ronny "Head" Drayton, and Greg "Ionman" Tate.

Thanks to the countless master musicians and bands I've worked and associated with these last four decades, too many to give account here. And my eternal gratitude to Gene Williams and all iterations of the BRC Orchestra for uplifting our Black rock champions.

My Santa Barbara folk—Limon and Limon-extended Family, Torres Family, Nix-Bradleys & Soul Bites, Shalhoob Family, James Joyce III, Jordan Killebrew, Sarah York-Rubin, Hannah Rubalcava, Santa Barbara Arts Advisory Council, Santa Barbara Trust For Historic Preservation–thanks for making a Brooklyn kid feel at home.

Thanks to my legal counsel, Greg Thomson, for the advice and the deep chats.

To my brother in all things except biology, Vini Miranda, for forty-seven years of brotherhood. All my gratitude, you already know—there's nothing more I can add.

It is only through the passion of my wife, Sally A. Foxen-McNeill—my love, my rock, my counsel—that I've been able to find my way to my truest self. Thank you, beloved, for your unwavering love and faith. I love you beyond measure.

To the McNeill/Stewart families, blood and extended, thank you for shaping the man I am. To my godmother,

Audrey Meyers—as my second mother, I hold you in reverence. To my sister Tracy and brother Kyle—the two of you are my foundation; without you I cannot stand. Finally, to my late parents, Martin and Carabelle McNeill, all my achievements, the man I've become, are through your influence and guidance. Everything I am, I owe to you both. I only wish you were here to see it.

Finally, of course, I have to thank the Isleys, Ronald, Ernie, and Chris Jasper and their extended families. Not only has your music set a bar of excellence, it's been a beacon guiding many Black musicians like me past the sinister lie about Black people having "no place in rock and roll." Thank you for reminding the world, in spite of all the "bullshit" thrown at you/us, that Black people have ownership stake in *every single thing* authentic and legitimate about rock and roll.

Blessed and well-earned rest to the Isleys in paradise: O'Kelly Sr., Sallye Bernice, O'Kelly Jr., Rudolph, Vernon and Marvin.

Introduction

**The Isley Brothers Are America's Most Tenured
Rock and Roll Group: Deal with it.**

All you are ever told in this country about being Black is
that it is a terrible, terrible thing to be. Now, in order to
survive this, you have to really dig down into yourself and
recreate yourself, really, according to no image which yet
exists in America. You have to decide who you are, and
force the world to deal with you, not with its *idea* of you.
—*Interview with Studs Terkel from "Conversations with
James Baldwin" (1989)*[1]

I try to play my music, they say "The music's too loud"/
I try talking about it, I got the big runaround/
And when I rolled with the punches, I got knocked to the
ground/
By all this BULLSHIT goin' down . . .
—*from "Fight the Power," The Isley Brothers (1975)*[2]

The following statement is made with full expectation of
derision and backlash in pop culture's Kangaroo Court

of Entrenched Sociological Retrograde. Any offense taken does *nothing whatsoever* to mitigate from amply evident truth: to wit, The Isley Brothers are, indisputably, America's longest-tenured, most venerable, active rock and roll group. Not R&B, nor funk, nor soul group. *Rock and roll* group.

This is *not* hyperbole. This is *not* opinion. This is an uncontestable *fact*. Let it be said again. Loudly. For the haters, the cynics, the hard-headed, the tone deaf, and so all the folks in the back and up in the cheap seats can hear: The Isley Brothers are, *indisputably*, America's longest-tenured, most venerable, active ROCK AND ROLL GROUP. Not R&B, nor funk, nor soul group. Again: ROCK AND ROLL GROUP.

Deal with it.

Music and culture do not manifest in a societal vacuum, no matter how angrily we demand it to be so. That fiction leads down a road of misguided denial of the creators' experiences, the audiences they touch, and the gravitas of their work. This book, about music, is equally about culture, society, politics, and race, and how these factors shape the music and how it is received (or not). All things being subjective, one person's Nat King Cole is another's William Hung, but the context in which such ideas are formulated and how they are framed weigh just as heavily as their gist.

One crucial root cause of disconnect stems from hardwired biases ingrained in the national psyche, most acutely evinced when navigating the fault lines of race and culture. These schisms are intensified when businesses and media inform themselves, disseminate, and exploit these biases without scrutiny, even in the face of empirical evidence. Innumerable truths are strangled from decades of indoctrination, unilateral propagandizing, reductive classifications, and calculated obliviousness, making any coherent discourse among disparate groups impossible.

This book attempts to open such a discourse about the Isleys' venerable work, their history, and contributions to the culture, underscoring how the industry and social bias effectively *minimize* Black groups like The Isley Brothers. There's a historic vacuum in open dialogue, analysis, and evaluation of these acts in the pop canon, *made keenly plain* given the Isleys' transgenerational influence and evergreen success. As one of the most successful artists (Black or otherwise) in history, they are a case study on how race and culture inform how music is absorbed into the American consciousness.

The Isleys by the Numbers

For all the folks who demand receipts, these are a few of the benchmarks from the Isleys' portfolio: their first official recording, "Angels Cried" on Teenage Records, was released in 1957—a year after rock and roll's 1956 explosion, where Elvis Presley exposed this underground world of Black music, once classified "rhythm and blues," to the masses. The Isleys shuffled around a deluge of indie labels (Teenage, Gone, End, Wand, etc.) before scoring the million-selling "Shout" on RCA in 1959, making them legitimate stars alongside legions of pioneers like Little Richard, Chuck Berry, Bo Diddley, LaVern Baker, and Fats Domino.

The Isleys had million-sellers in 1961 with "Twist and Shout," and in 1966 with "This Old Heart of Mine." They launched Jimi Hendrix to stardom. Their songs have been covered by icons like The Beatles, The Doobie Brothers, The Yardbirds, Whitney Houston, and Robert Palmer. Their anthem, "It's Your Thing," won a Grammy in 1970. Alongside original hits like "Freedom," "Lay Away," and "Work to Do," they boast rich reinterpretations of rock standards, like "It's Too Late," "Lay, Lady, Lay," "Fire and Rain," even scoring a Top Ten hit with Steven Stills' "Love the One You're With."

In the 1970s, the Isleys had ten successive gold, platinum, or double platinum albums: *Givin' It Back*; *Brother, Brother, Brother*; *3+3*; *Live It Up*; *The Heat Is On*; *Harvest for the World*; *Go for Your Guns; Showdown*; *Go All the Way*; and *Grand Slam*. They were inducted by Little Richard into the Rock and Roll Hall of Fame in 1992. The Isleys have releases on *all three* major labels (Warner, Sony, and Universal), have charted hits in eight decades and Top 40 million-sellers in at least *six*. No other artist in *history*, Black, White, Purple, Plaid, or Polka Dot, can make that claim. In 2014, they won a Grammy Lifetime Achievement Award. Neil Strauss of the *New York Times* observed, "In the mercurial world of pop music, surviving while remaining relevant can be a form of genius. This makes The Isley Brothers . . . as close to genius as any other pop act."[3]

The group sold over 18,000,000 albums in the United States alone, with ten original albums shipping over one million units each. Their prime platinum run came at the Isleys' apex of rock-driven albums, starting with 1971's

Givin' It Back and peaking with 1978's *Showdown*, with over 7,060,000 units sold, all aligned with the rise of the AOR format. During this period (not counting live or greatest hits albums), the Isleys kept pace with or outsold The Beach Boys (6,701,260), Heart (6,624,440), John Lennon (6,427,000), Yes (6,175,107), George Harrison (5,960,000), Steely Dan (5,930,000), Deep Purple (5,908,000), Creedence Clearwater Revival (5,740,000), Eric Clapton (5,520,614), Van Morrison (5,401,000), Bachman Turner Overdrive (5,400,000), Emerson Lake & Palmer (5,263,480), Grateful Dead (5,100,000), Supertramp (4,657,000), Three Dog Night (4,604,980), The Moody Blues (4,200,000), Paul Simon (3,609,090), REO Speedwagon (3,500,000), Allman Brothers (3,047,680), Cheap Trick (2,249,840), Thin Lizzy (2,100,000), David Bowie (2,072,384), and many others.[4]

All this *without* the benefit of regular rotation at dedicated album-oriented rock radio, nor exposure in rock media outlets of the day, nor promoters who would present the band to so-called "core" rock audiences. Also, without urban/Black radio and media embracing the Isleys' rock pedigree, cherry-picking tracks suited for mainstream Black audiences and reflexively classifying their work as "funk" or "soul."

Ernie Isley, the band's guitarist, said, "They may not put us on some magazine cover, but people know our significance. The Beatles know. Jimi Hendrix knows. Berry Gordy knows. Todd Rundgren knows. Bob Dylan knows. The Doobie Brothers know. Biggie Smalls knows. Anybody who takes the time to examine our career will say, 'Obviously, these guys are the genuine article.'"[5]

Tenth Circle of Hell: "Black Famous"

There's a buzzword which doggedly surfaces in many "general market" (i.e., White) circles regarding the Isleys: "underrated." Howard Kramer, former curatorial director for the Rock and Roll Hall of Fame Museum: "The Isley Brothers are shockingly underappreciated . . . their records are every bit as good [as the Rolling Stones and Led Zeppelin]."[6] NPR TV critic Eric Deggans: "Ernie Isley should be right up there with Jimi Hendrix. But because [his] guitar solos were powering songs that were popular with Black people, White people never got hip to him."[7] James Porter, Chicago Reader: "One side of the Isley Brothers' career . . . consistently gets swept under the rug: their status as a hard-rock band. In the 1970s, the Isley Brothers made heavy metal you could dance to."[8] Jeff Terich, Treble Media: "There's a lot to hear in the Isleys' catalog, much of it familiar, some of it vastly underrated, but all of it worthy of resdiscovery."[9]

It seems inconceivable to have such a distinguished 67-year career and yet *still* be considered "underrated." In reality, most of rock's White stewards denied the Isleys a fair and equal hearing compared to their White peers. The penchant to dismiss Black performers from rock dissuaded incalculable fans from engaging the group at their peak. Overwhelmingly, Black pop fans kept the Isleys in the public discourse, but without the major payoff of "rock crossover" status. It's only now, via the internet, that listeners of all races and ages are catching up with the Isleys' music decades later. "Their story is much more the story of the segregation of music," Deggans said. "There's this long legacy of really amazing Black rock [musicians] that are sort of unknown because White audiences don't know them."[10]

The Isleys' one consolation is they have outlasted (if not outsold), virtually every White rock icon ever, and are still making relevant music. But this came at a cost of ostracization from lucrative scenes they helped foster, as well as forced reinvention to maximize their viability within so-called "traditional" Black genres with less economic and political bandwidth. The group (and many of their Black peers) need to be in the same conversations as The Beatles, The Stones, Led Zeppelin, and every significant White band of the classic rock era. But they are not, which begs the question: How does a Black rock artist who sells a million records have inherently less market value than a White rock artist who sells a million records? Who devises this nebulous standard of "White versus Black" aesthetics to which these systems and practices are forced to abide? And on what basis, given that *self-admitted* segregation allows neither side insight into genres/cultures outside of their chosen spheres?

The Isley Brothers epitomize dozens of Black rock artists—The Chambers Brothers, WAR, Shuggie Otis, Joan Armatrading, Labelle, Funkadelic, Billy Preston, Betty Davis, Mother's Finest, Mandrill, and others—forced to navigate the hazardous straits of capitalism and the myth of American homogeneity that pulls over and pats down Black innovation so White appropriation can proceed unencumbered. There are thousands of White acts who didn't sell half the records, have half the longevity, nor have half the influence as any of these Black artists, yet are more exalted within rock music.

3+3, The Album That Threatened to Change the Game

These biases posed near-insurmountable challenges for the Isleys. Summarily, one of most essential rock catalogs never got the spotlight it deserved—including the masterpiece that made the group an institution. The run-up to 1973 had afforded the Isleys a respectable, if not always consistent, fifteen-year career: a Grammy, four Top 40 hits, and twenty-one songs in the *Billboard* Top 100. But they lacked the watershed moment that would firmly ensconce them in the rock firmament. Then in July, the floodgates finally burst open: heralded by the classic "That Lady," *The Isley Brothers 3+3* firmly established the group among elite circles. It was the first of eight successive platinum albums; their career and legend thereafter solidified (*Billboard* Black albums #2; *Billboard* pop albums #8, two million copies sold, and twenty weeks on the charts).[11] It was a rare record by a Black act that hit urban, rock, and pop crowds equally, despite the chasm between Black and White formats and audiences. Even some AOR stations put it in rotation.

But the rock establishment threw every disqualifier at the Isleys, barely couched as "race-neutral" critique, oblivious to the paradox of White artists with sonically comparable work (Elton John, Leon Russell, Bachman-Turner-Overdrive, Hall & Oates, Credence Clearwater Revival, Bob Seger, Chicago, et al.). Eric Weisbard, critic, educator, and organizer of EMP Pop Conference, notes in his book *Top 40 Democracy: The Rival Mainstreams of American Music*:

> Rock definitionally excluded the Black performers central to an earlier era's rock and roll. Alice Nichols writes, "the

color line in popular music had reemerged and felt nearly as solid as the days before Chuck Berry and Little Richard broke through it." Artistry was irrelevant: "AOR listeners," Nichols bemoans, "would never know that black rock was not an oxymoron, that Nona Hendryx and Parliament-Funkadelic rocked with the best of them."[12]

The Isleys are still here, albeit through several incarnations and a fan base light-years removed from their rock heyday. Nearly all the White icons they influenced, and then were eclipsed by, are not. Even rock as a genre doesn't have the same social currency it had when "the powers that be" fought so ferociously to exclude them. "The way the business is," Ernie Isley said, "there's one microphone and everybody wants to get to the controls. Whoever gets there has the right to say whatever they wanna say. The Isley Brothers—our music and our career—are in the fine print, the details of whatever it is rock 'n roll is about. It's up to others to bring all of it to light."[13]

That is what this book is about, bringing all of those details to light. The Isley Brothers are, indisputably, America's longest-tenured, most venerable, active rock and roll group. Not R&B group. Not funk group. Not soul group. *Rock and roll* group. And we *really* need to deal with this . . . Some *way* more than others . . .

1
Climbing Up the Ladder
The Road from the Queen City to Teaneck, NJ

Lincoln Heights, OH—a suburb 13 miles north of Cincinnati, with a population of about 3,300 circa 2019—has the distinction of being the first Black self-governing community north of the Mason-Dixon Line. It was a product of the Great Migration, the mass exodus of 6,000,000 Black Americans escaping the repression of the Jim Crow South, to parts Northeast, Midwest, and West between 1910 and 1970. Lincoln formed out of restrictive zoning that prohibited Black home ownership within the Queen City proper, hewn from unincorporated land sold to these families in 1923.[1] Incorporation efforts in 1939 were blocked until 1946, after affluent bordering White communities—skittish at having an autonomous Black enclave adjacent—carved up surrounding areas, taking vital industries, until Lincoln was a tenth of its original size (one square mile).[2] This common practice exposed the myth of Northern states being less segregated than Southern states, despite no explicit discrimination laws. There were vastly greater opportunities, yes, but within firm, albeit tacit, parameters. Life for Black Americans in the North was—*is still*—only marginally less separate and unequal than the South.

It was there that a former naval officer from Durham, NC, O'Kelly Isley Sr., and his betrothed from Albany, GA, Sallye Bernice Bell, put down roots and set about raising six boys: O'Kelly Jr., Rudolph, Ronald, Vernon, Ernie, and Marvin. The father, a one-time vaudevillian, and the mother, pianist and organist for Mount Moriah Baptist Church, brought up their children in equal parts church and secular music. O'Kelly Sr. visioned his sons as the next iteration of another famous Ohio fraternal band, The Mills Brothers. The four oldest sang in church, groomed after Billy Ward and His Dominoes and The Dixie Hummingbirds. Winning contests like *Ted Mack's Original Amateur Hour*, the group barnstormed churches with their doting mother throughout Ohio, Kentucky, and the Eastern United States. "Our parents created the climate for us to learn about music when we were all very young," said Ronald. "They wanted us to have a complete musical education and they exposed us to everything."[3]

The group's story nearly ended, tragically, when 13-year-old Vernon was killed by a truck that struck him while riding his bike through the neighborhood. The group, inconsolable, disbanded temporarily. But after reflection and gentle persuasion of their parents, the surviving trio decided to regroup. Only now, they put down the gospel mantle and took up rock and roll, a huge risk as stars who blurred the gospel/rock meridian drew the ire of the church (Ray Charles, Sam Cooke, Aretha Franklin, Clyde McPhatter, etc.). Family patriarch, O'Kelly Sr., impressed upon his boys to persevere and pursue music even as he ominously predicted he wouldn't live to see their success—a harrowing decree so soon after Vernon's death. But, sure enough, "Senior" passed away from a heart attack two years later. So, on April 17, 1956, The Isley Brothers—Ronald, 15; Rudolph, 17; and O'Kelly, 18—made good on their father's premonition and took the leap of faith, setting off for The Big Apple.

The ten-hour Greyhound ride into the great unknown would have petrified such tender-aged dreamers, were it not for a fluke encounter with another passenger, prominent blues singer Beulah Bryant, who, upon being impressed by an impromptu audition from the boys, offered assistance. This was most fortuitous, because the group had little money and no place to stay. They took odd jobs, shuttling around town, eventually settling in Harlem. When they weren't working or making rounds near the Brill Building in Times Square— then the epicenter of the record business in New York, where legions of aspirant recording stars, musicians, songwriters, and producers converged hoping to catch their big break— the brothers rehearsed and hung out by The Apollo Theater. They even won the Wednesday Night Amateur contest.[4]

Bryant giving her young charges a leg up was a godsend, especially with legions of teen groups on the scene (Frankie Lymon & The Teenagers, Little Anthony & The Imperials, The Teenchords, etc.). One major connection was agent Nat Nazarro, who booked the Isleys at top Black-centered venues like DC's Howard Theatre, Philly's RKO Palladium, Chicago's Regal Theatre, and The Apollo, gigs that paid up to $950 a week. "We made more money than we ever made in our life," O'Kelly mused.[5]

These shows led the trio to sign to Teenage Records, founded by former singers Bill "Bass" Gordon (The Colonials) and Ben Smith (The Ben Smith Quartet). A single cut, "Angels Cried" b/w "The Cow Jumped over the Moon," was released in June 1957. It did well back in Cincinnati, but nowhere else. Unimpressed with lackluster sales, the group asked out of its contract but was refused. The brothers exited both the office and their deal in one fell swoop, with a bit of chicanery. "He left the contract on the desk and we picked it up [and walked out]," O'Kelly recounted, "I imagine he tore his whole office apart looking for his contract."[6]

The Isleys' next stop was Gone Records, helmed by George Goldner and Richard Barrett, two of the most important men of the early rock and roll era. Goldner founded several critical labels, such as Gee, Roulette, End, and Gone. With Barrett developing talent, the two discovered and delivered hits for young stars like Frankie Lymon & The Teenagers, Little Anthony & The Imperials, The Chantels, The Flamingos, and The Four Seasons. This was a double-edged sword: on the one hand, the Isleys were working with rock's busiest hit-making team; on the other, they didn't get the focus needed to boost a group if they didn't score hits out the box—and the Isleys weren't.

"They had a funny way of recording back in those days," O'Kelly recalled. "The studios were working the full 24 hours and they would bring in maybe ten groups and record enough tunes for dozens of discs."[7] The Isleys cut seven sides with Gone Records or its subsidiaries, with four singles all failing to chart. When they asked for their release in 1958, there was no ill will nor hard feelings. It was just as well in hindsight, considering Goldner's proximity to infamous label owner Morris Levy and his ties to organized crime. Goldner had a crushing gambling habit and sold his labels and artists to Levy to pay off his debts—he died of a heart attack in 1970 at 52.[8]

Next came RCA Records A&R Howard Bloom, who signed the group after catching one of their Philly sets. They were paired with legendary staffers Hugo Peretti and Luigi Creatore. The duo just arrived from a stint with Roulette, scoring hits for Jimmie Rodgers. Prior to that, they were at Mercury working with Sarah Vaughn and—put bluntly— "sanitizing" R&B records for White artists, notably Georgia Gibbs' "Dance with Me, Henry (Wallflower)" (Etta James), and "Tweedle Dee" (LaVern Baker). They leveraged a huge deal from RCA: guaranteed salary, a penny-per-album-sold royalty, and producer credit.[9] Hugo and Luigi were seeking a breakout smash, and fate dropped the brothers in their lap. The first single was "I'm Gonna Knock on Your Door." "It didn't do much," Ronald said. "We needed a hit."[10]

Then the brothers pitched an idea: they'd been closing shows with their take on Jackie Wilson's "Lonely Teardrops." As part of the routine, Ronald wound the song up reaching into their gospel days, stirring a rousing call-and-response built around the motif "You make me wanna SHOUT!" Typically making records suited for Sunday tea, "Shout" gave Hugo and Luigi a chance at something with more grit and grease. "They performed 'Shout' right there in the office a capella, with the choreography and everything," said Luigi Creatore. "We loved it, but the spontaneity, that magical live energy, was what it was all about. If the record sounds like a party, it was just that."[11]

The sessions were held late July 1959 at RCA Studios. In addition to the session players (including Isley organist Herman Stephens from Cincinnati), the group invited friends as an "audience" to capture the live show energy. The track ran over five minutes, a death wish for radio. But rather than edit or recut, they split the song in half, with Part 1 on the A-side and Part 2 on the B-side—a risk, but the fire remained intact.[12]

"Shout" was released weeks later, landing at #47 on the *Billboard* Top 100, the first Isley single to make the national charts—church groups pressured stations not to play it because of the song's gospel bent. "Shout" gave the Isleys juice to continue after grinding two years. And keeping the publishing under their company, Three Boys Music (a rarity for newcomers—especially *Black* newcomers), meant steady income. The Isleys bought houses in north New Jersey, including one in Englewood—near Clyde McPhatter, Sylvia Robinson (Mickey & Sylvia), and Drifters managers George and Faye Treadwell—where they moved mother Sallye, brothers Ernie and Marvin, and also used for a rehearsal space.[13] Chris Jasper (younger brother of Rudolph's wife, Elaine) would follow later. For three Black boys not old enough to legally drink, this was a big deal.

Sadly, "Shout" was a one-and-done deal. Follow-up singles—"Respectable," "How Deep Is the Ocean"—and the album *Shout* got no further momentum. And, typical of the time, White acts covering Black singles—Joey Dee & The Starliters (#6, 1962)—charted higher and sold more than the originals. While Hugo and Luigi plied their swag from "Shout" to snatch Sam Cooke for RCA, producing hits for him, The Tokens, Ray Peterson, Perry Como, and Elvis Presley,[14] the Isleys left RCA in 1961.

The group landed at Atlantic Records, founded in 1947 by Ahmet Ertegun (son of the first Turkish ambassador to the United States) and Herb Abramson (a dentistry student who worked part-time as an A&R/producer for National Records), both devotees of jazz, blues, and rhythm and blues. They signed the biggest names in Black pop: Ray Charles, The Drifters, The Coasters, LaVern Baker, Big Joe Turner, Shelley Manne, Leadbelly, Ruth Brown, and others. Abramson's wife, Miriam, managed the business.[15]

When the Isleys arrived, Atlantic was juggling twelve years of hand-to-mouth success. After buying out Abramson, who was doing a hitch in the Army, Ahmet took over leadership, hard-assed ex-*Billboard* staffer Jerry Wexler ran productions, and Ahmet's brother, Nesuhi, ran the jazz division. Abramson also divorced Miriam, bringing home a pregnant girlfriend who became his second wife. Miriam stayed at the company and married Freddy Bienstock, noted song whisperer for Elvis Presley. Ray Charles and Bobby Darin, accounting for a third of the label's income, defected not long before the Isleys signed. The arrival of hitmaker Solomon Burke and a distribution deal with a tiny Memphis label called Satellite Records—soon to be Stax—eased some of the pain. "We used to have to sell 60,000 singles in a week to meet the nut," said Wexler. "I remember every week, Ahmet and I and Miriam used to sit with a little hand crank adding machine to see if we survived that week."[16]

The Isleys were teamed with Hall of Fame production duo Jerry Leiber and Mike Stoller, authors of hits for rock and roll royalty (The Coasters, The Drifters, Big Mama Thorton, Elvis, etc.). Atlantic released four singles that all stiffed—in fact, a re-entry of "Shout" on the charts topping at #94 posted higher than any new Atlantic release. The group moved on with nary an acknowledgment from the label.

Next stop was Wand Records, a subsidiary of Scepter Records, founded by Florence Greenberg, housewife-turned-powerhouse record executive—like Miriam Bienstock, one of a scant few women on the scene. Greenberg learned the trade by taking a job with Miriam's now-husband, Freddy Bienstock, who was a family friend. She easily took to the profession, soon striking out on her own, starting four labels. Greenberg managed the business side, while songwriter/producer (and one-time paramour) Luther Dixon groomed talent as A&R and in-house producer. She launched stars like The Shirelles, Chuck Jackson, Jimmy Reed, The Kingsmen, Dionne Warwick, Maxine Brown, and B. J. Thomas. When the Isleys arrived, the label had just moved into the Brill Building, accessing a skyscraper full of creatives who helped them craft some of pop's most enduring records. Among them was hard luck song plugger-turned-producer Svengali Bert Berns. Berns produced jewels such as "A Little Bit of Soap," "I Want Candy," "Piece of My Heart," and "Hang on Sloopy."[17]

The initial session was rocky: the group had first crack at pop maestro Burt Bacharach's classic "Make It Easy on Yourself," but Dixon altered the title and lyrics to "Are You Lonely by Yourself," a heresy, given Bacharach's legendary fastidiousness. Ronald recalled, "Burt came in the studio and said, 'That's not my song! Who changed the words?' Well,

Luther had changed the words. There was a big argument, it lasted for a good hour and a half to two hours."[18] Bacharach pulled the piece outright. (As an aside, soul legend Jerry Butler heard the demo—sung by Dionne Warwick—and flew in to cut it with Bacharach, hitting #20 on the *Billboard* Hot 100 and #18 on the R&B chart.)

Meanwhile, "Bronx" Bert, whose session was scheduled right behind "Forest Hills" Burt, was livid, because his studio time was eviscerated, having only fifteen minutes to cut. A year prior, Berns suffered a similar abuse as Bacharach nearly did: Atlantic boss Jerry Wexler placed a Berns song on The Top Notes, a long-forgotten R&B duo. Wexler lorded over the session, which was "supervised" by the new hotshot producer Phil Spector. It was a spastic trainwreck of vocal hiccups, jerky angular rhythms, and nonlinear chord structure—Berns was horrified but powerless under Wexler's iron fist. "Twist and Shout" died an unlamented death ("You fucked it up," his exact words to Wexler).[19] In the Isleys, Berns saw its resurrection and a chance to give the finger to Spector and Wexler—it took some convincing, but the Isleys gave him his chance.

Smoothing the groove into a loping mambo back beat, swaggering horns, Ronald's assured lead, and adding a tension-building bridge out of an ascending chromatic vocal passage, the new version brought a funk alien to the Atlantic version. It was dynamite on wax, and record buyers responded: the single rocketed up *Billboard*, peaking at #17 on the Hot 100 in 1962 and #2 R&B, with a five-month chart run. The Isleys finally cracked the Top 20 with a bona fide rock anthem. Supreme affirmation came from The Beatles performing it in their live set and recording it for their first EP—it reached #2 on *Billboard* in 1964. Paul McCartney said in the Berns documentary, "The Isleys' version just blew our minds. This was a great song to perform."[20] But, again, the Isleys couldn't get any traction on follow-up singles. The song was a windfall for Bert Berns—$90,000 from The Beatles alone—and he would collaborate with the Isleys again, but with no other hits, the Isleys were on the move once more.

They didn't go far—inside the Brill Building were the offices of United Artists (UA) Records, a label founded by the legendary studio through Max Youngstein in 1957 to develop soundtracks. UA launched a rock and roll/R&B division and hired Leiber and Stoller, the Isleys' former Atlantic collaborators, to run it (the two were fired in a dispute with Jerry Wexler over royalties). With Berns also there, the transition was seamless. But there were still no hits: six singles (including "Who's That Lady") fizzled and the album *Twisting and Shouting*, by "The Famous Isley Brothers," was DOA.

At this point, the Isleys had to reassess: they weren't having chart success and hadn't been on any label longer than a year—the logical conclusion was to do their own. Record labels were set up like lemonade stands in the Wild West days of rock music—anyone had as much chance as any other of being successful. Ronald was made president, Rudolph vice president, and O'Kelly treasurer and business manager. Ronald's new hometown was chosen as the label name and T-Neck Records was born.

The trio kept as much of their operations in-house as possible, including using their touring band, The I.B.

Specials, as studio musicians. Early on, their guitarist quit and the group needed a replacement. Tony Rice, a friend of the Isleys, raved about a blazing young gunslinger who'd been scuffling around between chitlin circuit gigs, with high-octane solos and playing a right-handed guitar lefty. "I said, 'Aw, come on, man, he can't be that good,'" Ronald recalled. "I named all the guitar players I knew we'd like to have in our band. Tony said, 'He's better than any of them.'"[21]

An audition was arranged at the Isleys' New Jersey home studio. That afternoon, with nothing but a guitar case full of everything he owned *except a guitar* (he pawned it for food money), James Marshall Hendrix arrived at their doorstep. Skepticism was kept at bay long enough for them to hand him one—he then tore through their hits, including fiery takes on "Shout" and "Twist and Shout." There were no qualms at this point—Jimmy (not yet Jimi) was in the band. He was afforded favored nation status over the rest of The I.B. Specials: they not only got his guitar out of hock, but it was in such bad shape that they bought him a brand-new white Fender Stratocaster—what became his signature ax. He also took a spare room in their Englewood home.

Hendrix was a pure gentleman in the Isley house, Sallye taking to him like another son. He grew close to the younger boys, watching TV together, even catching the world-shattering Beatles debut on Ed Sullivan with the family. There was vague foreboding as the Isleys saw rock's future laid bare: The Beatles' popularity signaled a change of the guard, galvanizing a stampede of aspirant (White) rockers into guitar shops—a genre that never treated Black artists fairly would only get worse now. O'Kelly was unmoved:

"'They got two guys on guitar,'" Ernie recounts him saying. "'*But we got Jimmy!*'"[22] This intimacy was critical, especially for young Ernie, then 11, as he had a front-row seat to the guitar god's practices, work ethic, and listening habits—Muddy Waters, The Three Kings (Albert, Freddie and B.B.), Curtis Mayfield, and T-Bone Walker. Hendrix may not have given hands-on tutelage, but he provided Ernie a foundation.

Hendrix on the road was a different beast—he was every bit the wild man he was hired to be: combustible solos, wild theatrics, and outrageous style. He upstaged the band, and, at times, the Isleys themselves. The group were adherents of R&B tradition: drill team choreography, precision performance, pristine grooming. This regimen was anathema to Hendrix—he wore bright scarves and bracelets in defiance of the dress code. "If our shoe laces were two different types," he said, "we'd get fined five dollars [out of $30 a night pay]. Oh, man, did I get tired of that."[23] The tour grind also wore on the guitarist: "I got tired of playing in the key of 'F' all the time."[24] He wrecked the band station wagon after hitting a deer driving from a gig. He missed one show entirely hooking up with an old girlfriend after a date in his hometown of Seattle.

After touring for months, the Isleys booked a studio in the spring of 1964 to record their first T-Neck single, "Testify." The song employed many of the gimmicks used in "Shout," a church revival feel with a "live" audience, dramatic breakdowns, and an ascending vocal section—as the song ran six minutes, it was even cut in half. The key difference is the infusion of Hendrix's rifling licks throughout and a short

solo midway. Sadly, like all of the group's recent output, the record was a dud.

By summer, Hendrix decided to part company. He gave his notice at a stop in Nashville. "It got very boring," he said, "Because you get tired of playing behind people all the time."[25] Hendrix would cut tracks or tour with Little Richard, Don Covay, Wilson Pickett, King Curtis, and others, still scuffling around New York, doing pickup gigs, and leading his band, Jimmy James and The Blue Flames. He did a few more shows and two more tracks with the Isleys ("Move Over and Let Me Dance," "Have You Ever Been Disappointed") and stayed at their house until he left for good in 1965. He visited once more in 1967—this time officially as "Jimi Hendrix," after his career exploded—on a quick "hello" before heading out for his defining performance at Monterey Pop. It was the last time the Isleys saw their adopted brother.

The group was still challenged with getting traction for their T-Neck releases. They gamely returned to Atlantic and signed a distribution deal, including the new singles with Hendrix—all three tanked. This time, the group was brusquely dropped. They made a last-ditch effort to reconnect with United Artists, landing on its subsidiary, Veep. They cut "Love Is a Wonderful Thing." And, again, no dice.

Four years passed since the Isleys had a chart hit. It was also seven years after an acquaintance from Teenage Records, a songwriter once a Brill regular, started killing the game with his own label. He wrote hits for LaVern Baker, The Falcons, and their favorite, Jackie Wilson (including their former closer, "Lonely Teardrops"). It couldn't have been lost on them that another Black son of the Midwest was enjoying

vast success from the comfort of his Detroit home. They called to gauge interest and Berry Gordy Jr. was all too happy to sign them—the Isleys were on their way to Motown.

2648 West Grand Boulevard, a.k.a. "Hitsville U.S.A.," an old house bought with a loan of $800 from his family (with a garage/kitchen combo converted into a recording studio), was Gordy's base of operations. From this humble edifice, a thousand pop standards were launched, along with many iconic performers: The Miracles, The Four Tops, Stevie Wonder, The Temptations, The Supremes, Marvin Gaye, and countless others. Motown had a deep pool of talent, making the Isleys' arrival a sore point for acts "waiting their turn." The vibe was uneasy, but the brothers were eager to get hits and learn the business. They patrolled the campus seeking collaborators, but with the high volume of hits the label demanded (110 Top 10s from 1961–71), quality time with top producers was inaccessible for newcomers or outsiders—the Isleys were both.

They finally caught a break, as Eddie Holland had a piece Holland-Dozier-Holland had written with Sylvia Moy. According to Lamont Dozier, "Ronnie and them had been practically beggin' for songs. It was an exercise song I used to play on the piano all the time. Eddie finished it, and then we took it to [the Isleys] to stop them from buggin' us."[26] The Isleys and Holland-Dozier-Holland set up to conjure the magic for what became "This Old Heart of Mine (Is Weak for You)." "Heart" has all the earmarks of an HDH classic, a bouncing groove from Benny Benjamin and James Jamerson, a rollicking stride piano from Earl Van Dyke, a lilting string arrangement from the Detroit Symphony Orchestra, a

signature honking baritone sax solo by Mike Terry, and call-and-response backing vocals from The Aldantes. But Ronald and the brothers ease in and caress the melody, raising the song through the stratosphere, as refined a performance as they'd ever done. Released in January 1966, "This Old Heart of Mine" made the nation sit up and take notice: peaking at #6 on the *Billboard* R&B charts and #12 on the *Billboard* Hot 100, the Isleys finally had another chart smash.

The single's success brought raw feelings to the workplace. At a Supremes' performance at New York's Copacabana, Gordy told the Isleys that Motowners were upset they "jumped the line." Regardless, the group had a top ten hit, which meant they needed an album to support it. *This Old Heart of Mine* was released in May with two follow-up singles: "Take Some Time Out For Love" and "I Guess I'll Always Love You." But nothing struck like the title track, and the rest of the album languished.

Then catastrophe struck Motown: Holland-Dozier-Holland—the label's A-team, authors of over 200 hit songs—were upset over discrepancies in their royalties and began a work slowdown, which trickled to a stoppage, then an outright exit.[27] This triggered back-and-forth litigation that lasted into the 1980s. Gordy countered by forming a unit called "The Corporation," an anonymous team of writers (Gordy, Freddie Perren, Deke Richards, and Fonce Mizell), to prevent undue notoriety for in-house writers. Another crew called The Clan—R. Dean Taylor, Frank Wilson, Pam Sawyer, and Richards again—also formed. Both teams cranked out songs for HDH acts, while everyone else hunkered down, as the company needed hits from whoever could deliver. Artists who weren't a major priority, like The Isley Brothers, were left in limbo.

A second Isley album, *Soul on the Rocks* (really a hodgepodge of songs), was released in January 1967. They covered Marvin Gaye's "That's the Way Love Is," and, in a full circle moment, the Jackie Wilson hit "Whispers (Gettin' Louder)." The only single was the Gaye cut—didn't chart. A non-album side, "Take Me in Your Arms," followed—didn't chart. "Behind a Painted Smile" was a hit in the UK—did nothing in the States. No higher up the Motown food chain, the next two years were squandered.

Another seismic tragedy with ties to the label shook the world: Dr. Martin Luther King Jr., human rights leader, was assassinated April 4, 1968, on the balcony of the Lorraine Hotel in Memphis. Gordy befriended King in 1963 during his "Great March To Freedom" to combat segregation practices in Detroit. He created the *Black Forum* label to document Black thought-leaders like King, Stokley Carmichael, Langston Hughes, and others. Motown recorded some of King's iconic speeches, with proceeds directed to designated organizations. Gordy attended King's funeral on April 9.

Despite mounting civil unrest and Black pop responding to it, Gordy was still disinclined to politicize Motown's music—he nearly pulled the plug on The Tempts' "Cloud Nine" and Marvin Gaye's "What's Goin' On?"[28] But the writing was on the wall: "Love Child," a Supremes song about an adult born out-of-wedlock, shipped #1 *Billboard* Hot 100, #2 *Billboard* R&B, #1 *Cashbox* Top 100 and R&B, #1 *Record World* 100 Top Pops and Top 50 R&B, two million copies sold, and three months on the charts. The Corporation had its first #1 on The Supremes without Holland-Dozier-Holland. Psychedelic soul overtook Motown, their output more dense, funky, complex, sophisticated: The Sound of Young America was finally growing up.[29]

The Isleys probably would have flourished from these changes, but they weren't in Motown's plans. Just as well, as the label's constraints were wearing on them, they wanted to express their own style. Also, the Isleys made a tour of the UK and were overwhelmed by the adulation they received, which gave them the confidence to venture out on their own. In November 1968, the brothers asked for their release, which Gordy granted amicably (at least, *at the time*. This would loom later). In an odd twist, the Isleys departed just as Motown signed yet another band of Midwest Black brothers—by way of Gary, IN—who would be the first test of The Corporation's mettle. They would soon monopolize the company's attention, in exchange for one of Motown's most lucrative seasons and change the entire landscape of pop.

This also loomed later, but, now, not a concern for the Isleys, as the Motown chapter closed—the new chapter of T-Neck was starting.

2
It's Our Thing
T-Neck Records 2.0 and Becoming The Isley Brothers

By the end of 1968, America was profoundly transformed compared to 1958. The United States was mired in Cold War saber-rattling and the Vietnam Conflict. Outward boundaries of segregation softened, while internal structural impediments hardened. Manufacturing began its mass exodus out of the United States for cheaper goods and labor. The Civil Rights Movement splintered—some elements assimilating, others radicalizing—while other human rights struggles (women, LatinX, indigenous peoples, LGTBQIA, anti-war) pushed their way onto the world stage. America's drug use behind closed doors spilled out into the open. Upheaval in big cities became routine. Four assassinations on American soil—Dr. King, Malcolm X, John, and Robert Kennedy—fomented disquiet. The reactionary xenophobia of the 1950s whipsawed into the Free Love zeitgeist of the 1960s, which began dissipating into the ennui and alienation that gripped the 1970s. Television gave a front-row seat to a nation's dissociative breakdown.

Rock and roll, now no longer in the closet, both documented and informed these societal transformations. Indeed, the genre itself had transformed—expression had expanded, becoming less constrictive, bolder, more experimental, diverse, and original. The British Invasion, Motown, Chicago electric blues, San Francisco Flower Power, Laurel Canyon hippie, Memphis soul, Greenwich Village folk, Detroit edge, Southern rockabilly, downtown avant-gardists, New Orleans funk, Sunset Strip thrash, East Village proto-punk, and other movements—driven by indie songwriters and artist/composers—broke the iron grip of Tin Pan Alley, The Brill Building, and Hollywood studios on popular music. The material emanating from these new sources spoke to the issues and tenor of the times and ultimately usurped the old school system.

Here, the Isleys went back to the drawing board. However, unlike previous success/failure cycles, they now had invaluable lessons. A little older and wiser, the Isleys resurrected T-Neck. Having worked inside the most successful independent label in the country—founded and run by a Black man, no less—the idea of them achieving something similar wasn't so far-fetched. "During our three years [at Motown] we learned everything," Ronald said. "We increased our knowledge many times over. We feel that now we have our chance to go out and do things the way we want to."[1]

The Isleys were determined to control as much of the company as possible—the creative process, the production, and the publishing. They sought to forge their own distinct style, as well as the freedom to be responsive to change, unlike Motown, which was often accused of being highly regimented (Ernie quipped, "Motown was like, '*Ten-shun!* Record!'").[2] This meant leveling-up their songwriting and their business. The trio opened a new publishing company— Triple 3 Music, Inc.—to manage their songs. "We want to do our own thing on records," O'Kelly said of the relaunch of T-Neck. "We have a sound that is new, and we want to do it all on our own."[3]

As the front man, Ronald was spokesperson for the group. O'Kelly, the oldest, was the boss and handled all the business— his word was law. Rudolph was the enforcer, reputed to carry a licensed pistol, in the nefarious world of shady bookers and promoters, to ensure the Isleys got paid promptly and in full (legend has it Rudolph qualified for an open-carry license through FBI training).[4] The brothers also groomed the youngsters—Ernie (guitar, drums), Marvin (bass), and Chris Jasper (keyboards)—to come into the family business. Jasper, who moved into the Isleys' New Jersey home/HQ to attend Julliard briefly, said, "We formed a trio, The Jazzmen. We played just about anywhere we could. The older guys used to watch us rehearse, come to some of our gigs. As we got better, they wanted us to play with them."[5] It would be a while as Ernie and Marvin had to finish high school, then later joined Chris at C.W. Post College in Brookville, NY, to study music and business.

The Isleys needed a distribution partner more aligned with their business plan than previous efforts. The T-Neck imprint ultimately landed on Buddah Records in 1969, a New York independent founded two years earlier. Buddah was born from Kama Sutra, a subsidiary of MGM Records, founded by Art Kass, a respected label veteran. Buddah's most important figure, however, was an ambitious 24-year-old former Cameo-Parkway VP of sales, named Neil Bogart. Bogart was the whiz kid who would go on to launch the quicksilver Casablanca Records empire.[6]

Under Kass and Bogart, Buddah established itself hawking novelty records and "bubblegum pop," but eventually signed some of music's most important artists and put out some of pop's most iconic records. Alongside 1910 Fruitgum Company, The Lemon Pipers, and The Ohio Express, the label signed or distributed the works of The Lovin' Spoonful, Melanie, Captain Beefheart & His Magic Band, The Five Stairsteps, The Edwin Hawkins Singers, Bill Withers, Gladys Knight & The Pips, and Curtis Mayfield. With a solid company behind them, the Isleys were poised for success. All they needed were hits—and they already had one in the bag.

In late 1968, around the time the Isleys either left or were leaving Motown—this timing figures heavily for the group shortly—a song came to Ronald while driving his daughter to school. He had to keep humming to remember it when he got to his mother's home to write it down. He had some of the lyrics and finished it with Rudolph and O'Kelly, both affirming they did, indeed, have a hit on their hands. They reportedly booked time at A&R Studios in New York in January of 1969, using members of Wilson Pickett's road band, noted Memphis guitarist Skip Pitts on lead guitar, altoist George Patterson writing the charts, and a nervous 16-year-old Ernie Isley on bass after the session bassist failed to capture the feel the song had in rehearsals.[7]

The track "It's Your Thing" was released a little over a month after completion and was an immediate smash. It had grit and grease for years, with a swaggering rhythm section, Pitts' funky guitar hook, robust piano counterpoint, a sassy call-and-response horn chart, and the return of Ronnie's signature vocal style, alternating between sultry purr and ferocious roar. The song was attuned to the revolutionary sounds of the day, serving as an ode to independence and originality. It spoke for the Black power, hippie, women's liberation, gay rights, and other movements, while not bound to any. The Isleys didn't just have a hit record—they crafted a generational American anthem: "It's Your Thing" dominated the first half of 1969, reaching #2 on *Billboard* Hot 100, #1 R&B, and stayed on the charts for twenty-one solid weeks.

The debut album, *It's Our Thing*, was as audacious as the single, particularly its cover. Gone was the gassed hair that defined Black groups of the doo-wop era. Gone were uniform slick suits. Gone were the ambiguous images that either muted or camouflaged racial identity. Here were three serious Black men in bold Technicolor, crowned by perfectly coiffed Afros, dripped in robes of leather and fur, bright shirts and vests, staring proudly, *defiantly*, into the camera. The subtext was unmistakable: "You have never seen brothers (hereditary and/or cultural) like this before. Deal with it."

"It's Your Thing" heralded 1969 as a watershed year for pop music, where top artists across all genres released pinnacle, career-defining works, breaking boundaries and redefining themselves and the entire musical landscape. The Isleys' gamble was already paying dividends: their biggest hit to date; a sold-out, self-financed concert filmed at Yankee Stadium, featuring the Isleys, The Five Stairsteps, The Edwin Hawkins Singers, Moms Mabley, Ike & Tina Turner, and others (The Isleys were so well-received, a huge crowd stormed the stage and security had to form a human barricade around the band); and "It's Your Thing" went on to sell two million copies, and won the group its only competitive Grammy, Best R&B Vocal Performance by a Duo or Group in 1970.

Sadly, like every success the Isleys had, a setback was in the offing, this time from an unexpected source: Berry Gordy, Jr. Gordy was notoriously disinclined to allow big money to walk off the Hitsville campus without a fight. He fought the departure of his then-biggest star, Mary Wells, who, discontent with her royalty payments, had her contract voided when she turned 21. He was already embroiled in a breach-of-contract suit with Holland-Dozier-Holland. He fined members of The Funk Brothers for taking sessions off-book from Motown. The prospect of a former act that hadn't had a hit in over two years resurfacing with the year's biggest just two months after jumping ship seemed entirely too implausible—and apparently didn't sit well with the chairman.

Motown filed a breach-of-contract suit which claimed: (a) the Isleys were still under contract to Motown when "It's Your Thing" and two other songs were recorded, (b) the company had advanced $1,000 to the group for this purpose, and (c) Jobete Music Co. (Motown's publishing arm) and Motown retained ownership of the masters and the publishing over Triple 3 Music and Buddah. There was a lot of intrigue and shifting sands about when the group's release was final, where and when the recording was actually done, what money changed hands and what it was used for, and where the master tapes were (one deposition stated Sallye Isley unwittingly threw them out).[8] Although Motown sued twice (1969 and 1975), the court found in favor of the Isleys.[9] Not like Motown was put out: the drama didn't keep the label from placing "It's Your Thing" on The Temptations, The Supremes & The Four Tops jointly, and The Jackson 5. The Isleys continue to credit Motown for their success and appeared at a MusicCares benefit for Gordy and Smokey Robinson in 2023.

Not wanting to lose momentum, the Isleys were back in studio to work on the new album, *The Brothers: Isley*. This would be the recording debut of all three newcomers—Ernie on guitars and drums, Chris on keyboards, and Marvin on bass. They were still in school and not full band members yet, but these were first steps. George Patterson returned on alto and horn arrangements, and assorted musicians did the rest. The first single, "I Turned You On," did well, landing #23 on *Billboard* Hot 100 and #2 R&B. It was an unabashed return to the chunky groove of "It's Your Thing." Two other singles, "The Blacker The Berrie" and "Was It Good to You," never cracked above #29 R&B or #79 pop. The album reached #20 R&B and #180 pop—not the lofty perch of *It's Our Thing*, but still, two charting albums in a row was no small feat.

The year 1970 started auspiciously with the 11th Annual Grammy Awards at the Century Plaza Hotel in Los Angeles on March 12. The Isley Brothers received their award just four days after they released their third T-Neck album, *Get into Something*. Its first single, "Bless Your Heart" (another crib from "It's Your Thing"), was released in late 1969.

Work began toward the year's end, and credited personnel included "Skip" Pitts (guitar), Truman Thomas (organ), Everett Collins (keyboards), George Moreland (drums), and George Patterson on alto sax and arrangements. Ernie, on bass, was the only new member credited, although the group maintained all three younger members played on all T-Neck material. In addition to "Bless Your Heart," five other singles were released off the album, with "Freedom" as the highest tracking cut off the album (#16 R&B, #72 pop). The album didn't storm the charts, but it charted—the third straight to do so. Independence didn't bring world domination, but it brought consistency.

An otherwise productive year ended on a tragic note: on September 18, 1970, Jimi Hendrix, guitar demigod whom the Isleys put on the map, died at St. Mary Abbott's Hospital in Kensington, West London, at 12:45 AM. His unresponsive body was found by EMTs in the flat of his girlfriend, Monika Dannemann, at the Samarkand Hotel. The report stated he'd asphyxiated on his own vomit after passing out from a mixture of sleeping pills and alcohol he took to help him sleep. Hendrix's meteoric ascent crash-landed a paltry four years after he was brought to UK soil. Ernie recalled getting the news: "Some guys in my school told me. I said, 'Man, you jivin'! I don't believe it!' I got home and O'Kelly sat me down. I said, 'Aw, *man*! Not *Jimi* . . .!"[10]

Hendrix's funeral was held October 1 at Dunlap Baptist Church in Seattle and he was buried at Greenwood Memorial Park in nearby Renton, WA. He is cited as one of the world's best guitarists, a sentiment echoed by Ernie Isley, who is often compared to his mentor. "Emotionally, he's my favorite," Isley said, "Because of what I saw and heard as an 11-year-old in my home. Everything everyone saw later after he left, I saw in my own bedroom. I knew before anyone else knew how great he was."[11]

Hendrix's station in the rock Pantheon remains indelible over half a century after his death, but his passing brought unforeseen consequences: with the popularization of FM radio and demographically separated formats, the cultural barriers for music solidified, segregating audiences by race, gender, age, region, and class, more so than music genre or style. Rock stations purged Black artists from their playlists and Black stations purged rock music. As the last emissary to traverse these barriers, Hendrix's death stifled any recognition of Black American culture—all that made a Jimi Hendrix possible—as the source material of rock. Radio analyst Ken Tucker explains, "[Album Oriented Rock] stations 'offered the kind of music their surveys told them appealed to—white males between the ages of thirteen and twenty-five.' The stations that played it consequently 'narrowed the very definition of rock and roll: by AOR guidelines, Black artists didn't play it, and neither did women.'"[12]

The Isleys and their peers were in an impossible position: when they first came on the scene, rhythm and blues *was* rock and roll. Black people lived it. White people were engaged in it vicariously. The industry cashed in. Fast forward twelve years, and quizzically R&B is no longer rock and roll, Black people are excised from the genre, and White people were ordained its sole arbiters and purveyors.[13] And the industry *still* cashed in. This is what made the Isleys' next album so curious: *Givin' It Back*, an album of reimagined rock covers, was a provocative reclamation of a genre the industry and its gatekeepers egregiously designate as foreign to Black people.

In a year flush with exemplary concept albums—*What's Goin' On, Fragile, Pearl, Freedom Flight, Imagine, Here Comes the Sun, There's a Riot Goin' On, The Low Spark of High Heeled Boys, Sticky Fingers, Music of My Mind, Led Zeppelin IV, Curtis,* and *Shaft*—*Givin' It Back* was conceptual, not just in content but in context. On its face, the proposition seemed simple: every T-Neck single was successful on the R&B charts but, except for "It's Your Thing" and "Black Berries," never got past #72 pop. At the same time, White artists enjoyed success covering Isleys' material—in most cases, charting higher than the originals. "It was a deliberate decision," said Chris Jasper. "Rock was taken from blues and R&B, so when people say we've gone into another type of music, they're wrong. All we are trying to do is use every facet of our musical knowledge and combine them into our new sound."[14]

The songs chosen for *Givin' It Back* were the best of the best from the best: Bob Dylan, James Taylor, Eric Burdon & WAR, Stephen Stills, Neil Young, labelmate Bill Withers, and departed friend Jimi Hendrix, all staples on the rock and pop charts. The personnel featured all the Next Gen Isleys, studio drummer George Moreland, and some session players. Bill Withers sat in on his composition, "Cold Bologna." All the songs were rock standards, crafted in singular Isley style: "Ohio/Machine Gun," "Fire and Rain," "Lay Lady Lay," "Spill the Wine," "Nothing to Do but Today," and "Love the One You're With." And the infusion of the younger Isleys provided a taste of the group's future sonic trajectory. The album is the richest, most textured, and refined they ever recorded at that time. It was the Isleys' first top-to-bottom masterpiece, the intrinsic definition of album-oriented rock. "We had done a few covers albums that were crucial," said Ernie, "because no one in Black music had bothered to do with White rock as White rockers had done to us by covering our songs."[15]

The cover art was similar, but oddly inverse to *It's Your Thing*, three Black men with Afros—a little rougher with age and experience—in Sepiatone, dressed in work clothes, holding acoustic guitars in front of a barn. Yet again staring proudly, *defiantly*, into the camera. The subtext, again, unmistakable: "You have never seen brothers (hereditary and/or cultural) like this before. Deal with it." The only question was who the challenge was being put to: White folks? Black folks? Both? The September 25 release—a year and a week after Hendrix died—provided a robust proof of concept. The first single, "Love the One You're With," blew up like wildfire, reaching #16 on *Billboard* Hot 100 and #3 R&B. "Spill the Wine" followed suit, peaking at #49 Hot 100 and #19 R&B. And "Lay, Lady, Lay" reached #29 R&B, #71 Hot 100. The album crossed radio formats: urban, progressive rock, Top 40 (even play from a few AOR stations), and charted very respectably—#13 R&B and #71 pop, their best showing since *It's Our Thing*. If it didn't shatter boundaries, *Givin' It Back* at least hinted at the possibilities.

While the Isleys were making crucial strides, their distribution partner, Buddah, was scuffling. Coming off a bountiful 1970 with ten hit singles, primarily from folk singer Melanie, and The Five Stairsteps' classic "Ooh, Child," the following years were stitched together by a few one-hit wonders and oddball flukes. Music journalist Bob Hyde wrote, "By 1971, progressive (album) rock had all but taken over the pop charts, both single and LP, and AM radio was becoming a bit of a 'Twilight Zone' in terms of programming. With little to offer in the rock area, Buddah and Kama Sutra would weather a bit of a hit drought for the next two years."[16]

The only consistently successful releases on Buddah came from its distribution partners: T-Neck, with The Isley Brothers; Sussex, home of Bill Withers, founded by industry legend Clarence Avant; Hot Wax, the new label by Holland-Dozier-Holland, with hit singing trio, Honey Cone; and Curtom, Curtis Mayfield's imprint. All four subsidiaries released huge albums and singles in the space of a year and were all that kept the label going. At some point money, promotion, and marketing resources would get stretched, depending on how hot a property was, and something was going to give.

The year 1972 may have been the breaking point—it was an even more of a monster year for the Buddah subsidiaries. Coming off a Grammy win for his million-selling gold folk-soul standard, "Ain't No Sunshine," Bill Withers continued his reign with the release of his next classic, *Still Bill*, which yielded two more signature tunes: "Lean On Me" (#1 pop *and* R&B, shipping in excess of three million units), and "Use Me" (#2 pop *and* R&B, shipping over one million units). Still, the biggest bonanza came from Curtis Mayfield and his apex soundtrack for *Superfly*: a rare #1 pop *and* #1 R&B album for weeks, with two Top Ten gold singles, "Freddie's Dead" (#2 R&B and #6 pop) and "Superfly" (#5 R&B and #8 pop). The album sold over twelve million copies and was nominated for four Grammys (winning a Hall of Fame Grammy in 1998).

Not like the Isleys phoned it in that year—their next album, *Brother, Brother, Brother*, continued the blueprint laid out with *Givin' It Back*, balancing exceptional covers with well-crafted originals. Ernie, Marvin, and Chris contributed both as players *and* as writers. Truman Thomas (organ) and George Moreland (drums) returned, and Karl Potter was brought in on congas. Tracks included three pieces by songwriting empress Carole King (fellow alumnus of The Brill Building): "Brother, Brother, Brother," "Sweet Seasons," and the group's take on her masterwork, "It's Too Late." Three of the five Isley originals were among their biggest hits: "Pop That Thing" (#3 R&B, #24 pop), "Lay Away" (#6 R&B, #54 pop), and "Work To Do" (#11 R&B, #52 pop). "It's Too Late," released in early 1973, didn't chart pop, but hit #39 R&B. Overall, the album went to #5 on the R&B charts, #29 on the pop charts. Aside from their debut, *Brother, Brother, Brother* was the Isleys' best effort—it just wasn't *Superfly* or *Still Bill*. Buddah was still dancing between raindrops and had no stars of its own to balance the ledger.

Two major developments drastically altered the nature of the relationship. First, Neil Bogart, the maverick who signed T-Neck and essentially ran Buddah, parted company in 1973. He and partner Cecil Holmes formed their own label—Casablanca Records—on the strength of a loan from Warner Brothers. When the Warners didn't deliver the promotional support he expected, Bogart played industry Three Card Monte for years, spending lavishly and staying just a hair's breadth ahead of collectors. Tens of millions in the hole, even after PolyGram bought into the label in 1977, Casablanca never became solvent until 1983, with the release of the *Flashdance* soundtrack (Bogart sold out in 1980 and died of cancer at 39 in May of 1982).[17]

Art Kass took over the day-to-day management of the Buddah roster—emphasis on "the *Buddah* roster." Kass was determined to bolster the main label and put his own stamp on it. He did so by pulling off the biggest coup in the record business that year: in February 1973, he signed legends Gladys Knight & The Pips, whose contract with Motown was up, promising the sun, the moon, the stars, and a few planets. They were given input on all their records, access to top producers, and the full weight of the promotional team. The group delivered multiple hits (including #1 pop and #1 R&B Grammy-winner "Midnight Train to Georgia"), and became the label's centerpiece.[18]

From the outside view, the optics didn't scan. The Isleys' main advocate jumps ship as their former labelmates swoop in and make roost—after they'd put in five years of sweat equity and turned in back-to-back major chart efforts. Unlike Curtom (where Mayfield obsessed about controlling his operations), or Sussex (which was run by a respected veteran), the T-Neck deal *specifically required marketing and promotion*. Whether this was in the Isleys' mindset or not, the idea of putting heart-and-soul effort into a release likely to get *less* support couldn't have been very appealing.

On an unspecified date in 1972, The Isley Brothers performed an intimate set at the landmark New York club, The Bitter End. This tiny, but hallowed, gin joint on Greenwich Village's Music Row launched such pop royalty as Bob Dylan, James Taylor, Linda Ronstadt, Richie Havens, Joan Baez, and Simon & Garfunkel. Many iconic live albums were recorded, including the Isleys' labelmate, Curtis Mayfield, who did his top-selling *Curtis/Live* performance there just the previous year.

The Isleys Live is a snapshot of a band about to enter a new stage of becoming itself. The group performed their most popular material from their T-Neck/Buddah run, the band comprising Ernie, Chris, and Marvin, drummer Neil Bathe, and percussionist Karl Potter. The album served as the "unofficial official" introduction of the younger siblings as full-time members of The Isley Brothers band. On the sorrowful blues-soul-rock elegy of "It's Too Late," O'Kelly proffers, "We had a very young guitar player with us, by the name of Jimi Hendrix. Jimi's not here anymore, but while he was with us, he inspired our youngest brother, Ernest Isley. We'd like to feature young Ernest now, on guitar . . ."[19] Released in March 1973, the disc sold well on the R&B chart (#14), while getting mired on the pop chart (#139).

The Isleys Live symbolized a beginning and an ending. It was a peek into the next stage of the band's progression— new members, new sound, new direction. It was also the culmination of five years of accomplishments falling just short—a relationship that had run its course and separation was imminent. Perhaps the earnestness in the group's rendition of "It's Too Late" was less lament than recognition. In any case, the message was clear: *The Isleys Live* was the last album the Isleys submitted to Buddah, effectively terminating their partnership.

3
3+3
Getting into Something

Founded on January 15, 1889, Columbia Phonograph
Company—now Columbia Records, a subsidiary of Sony
Music Corporation—is the oldest label in all of recorded
music. Its catalog boasts the most important recordings and
artists ever documented. But its history includes a checkered
correlation between Black music and its audiences.
Columbia's first artists were classical, and, except for one or
two blues acts with unimpeachable crossover appeal (and
almost as anthropological curation), Black pop performers
were mostly excluded from Columbia, placed on subsidiary
labels until the latter half of the twentieth century. In 1938,
William S. Paley and Columbia Broadcasting Systems (CBS)
bought Columbia's parent company; prior signees were
grandfathered; and the jazz roster evolved into the industry
standard. But as blues, rhythm and blues, and rock and roll
rose to prominence in the 1940s, no such acts were signed to
Columbia. Even two of Black pop's most strident advocates—
A&R/producers John Hammond (blues, rock and roll) and

George Avakian (jazz)—couldn't course-correct. This was Columbia's culture for nearly seventy-five years.

In the 1950s, this embargo was enforced by its top two men. First, Goddard Lieberson, a composer and producer of classical albums, came to Columbia as an A&R in 1938 and was appointed president in 1956. A graduate of Eastman School of Music in the 1930s, he supervised Columbia's award-winning classical and Broadway recordings and instituted all of its groundbreaking recording technologies. Second was the world-famous/infamous Mitch Miller, A&R, producer, bandleader, and TV personality. Miller also went to Eastman to study oboe and classical music, where he and Lieberson met and became lifelong friends. Miller went from playing with top orchestras for twenty years to A&R/producer of classical music at Mercury Records in the late 1940s, until coaxed to Columbia by Lieberson in 1950. Miller produced notable pop icons such as Johnny Ray, Patti Page, Doris Day, Percy Faith, Ray Conniff, Jo Stafford, Frank Sinatra, Dinah Shore, Rosemary Clooney, Tony Bennett, and Johnny Mathis.

Miller's contempt for rhythm and blues/rock and roll was palpable. He told *NME* in 1958, "Rock 'n roll is like musical baby food: it is the worship of mediocrity, brought about by a passion for conformity."[1] He also denounced payola and the influence of organized crime: "Everybody in the business knew what was going on. You had to pay to play."[2] Miller passed over Elvis Presley, Buddy Holly, and The Beatles. He actually offered Presley a contract but balked at Colonel Tom Parker's asking price, sending the "King of Rock and Roll" to RCA. Miller signed a young Aretha Franklin, who languished for five years until she famously took her talents to Atlantic Records in 1966.

Despite *literal millions* in sales walking out the door, Miller's non-rock edict was law. In his prime (during America's conservative atmosphere of the 1950s), his roster brought in a fortune. But as the 1960s arrived and rhythm and blues/rock and roll went mainstream, Columbia lost market share to independents, like Motown, Atlantic, Chess, Stax, Specialty, and others. Rock and roll exploded from 15.7 percent of the market in 1955 to 42.7 percent in 1959, with overall sales growth from $213 million to $603 million. With twenty-nine record firms now in competition versus seven in 1955, for a brief span, major labels lost half their market to independents.[3]

Two significant changes shifted Columbia's fortunes: first, in 1953, a new imprint was created—Epic Records— almost a catch-all label for artists not fitting Columbia's "brand." By the end of the 1960s, Epic earned gold records and became a force in rock and roll, R&B, and country, with a roster that included Sly & The Family Stone, Roy Hamilton, Bobby Vinton, The Dave Clark Five, The Hollies, Tammy Wynette, Donovan, The Yardbirds, Lulu, and Jeff Beck. Epic also managed distribution for other imprints, such as Okeh, Date, Philips, and later Stax and Philadelphia International. The second change was as low key as it was pivotal: a 26-year-old attorney joined the prestigious New York firm of Rosenman, Colin, Kaye, Petschek, and Freund in 1958. CBS was a client of partner Ralph Colin, who took the new associate under his wing. Within two years, the young attorney was hired as assistant counsel at Columbia

Records, and then general counsel the following year. That attorney was Clive Davis.

Born and raised in Crown Heights, Brooklyn, of working-class stock, Clive Jay Davis, "The Man with the Golden Ear," never so much as picked up a kazoo in his entire ninety-two years. Sheer providence and hard work landed him the job that made him pop music's most powerful man. Davis worked his way to the top of every setting, from Arista Honors Society in high school, to Phi Beta Kappa/magna cum laude at New York University, to Harvard Law and its Board of Student Advisors. He used the same drive to master the business, coupled with his innate musical taste. By 1965, Mitch Miller departed for MCA, and Davis was appointed administrative vice president and general manager. After a reorganization in 1966, he was tapped to run CBS Records.

"I had no ambition for it, and it was through lucky breaks that I got it," Davis told *Variety*. "I am eternally indebted to Goddard Lieberson for giving me the position and then, somehow, letting me do my thing—not that he knew I would have ears, or that *I* knew I would have ears."[4] Davis plunged into rock from the deep end, signing stars like Big Brother & The Holding Company (with Janis Joplin), Laura Nyro, The Electric Flag, Santana, The Chambers Brothers, Bruce Springsteen, Loggins & Messina, Blood Sweat & Tears, Aerosmith, Chicago, Pink Floyd, and Earth, Wind & Fire.

Black pop was still foreign country to Columbia, and Davis aggressively pursued correctives. In 1972, CBS commissioned Dr. Logan H. Westbrooks, the newly appointed director of Special Markets, and consultants from Harvard Business School to create "A Study of the Soul Music

Environment"—a.k.a. the infamous "Harvard Report"—to analyze strategies for CBS to penetrate the Black music market (this controversial document manifested unforeseen consequences for Black music later on).[5] CBS created a Black music division to sign, develop, market, and promote Black talent. The company also positioned Black artists on its subsidiaries, and signed distribution deals with independents, like Gamble & Huff's Philadelphia International in 1971, Stax in 1972, and, in May 1973, T-Neck Records—The Isley Brothers' new chapter began here.

Davis personally signed the Isleys, no doubt mindful of their pedigree. The Isleys sought CBS' muscle to take their career to the next level: larger production budget ($1-million advance for every album),[6] robust marketing and promotion, allowing them to make bigger, more creative moves. "We've now got the artistic avenue we've been looking for," Ernie said. "We are doing things now that most groups, particularly Black groups, have been limited in previously."[7]

The first major step was a change of scenery. Having recorded all their Buddah output at A&R Studios in midtown Manhattan, the Isleys went West for their first CBS project, setting up shop at the Record Plant in Hollywood, one of the premiere studios in the business. Opened in 1969 by Gary Kellgren and Chris Stone as a sister to their New York facility, it was designed not only as a state-of-the-art studio but adorned with extravagant creature comforts—bedrooms, lounges, dining rooms—traditional studios forsook for efficiency. Some of pop's most definitive music was created here: Fleetwood Mac's *Rumours*; The Eagles' *Hotel California*; Billy Joel's *Piano Man*; George Harrison's *Living in the Material World*; Crosby, Stills, Nash & Young's *So Far*; and countless others. It was also a nexus for networking, collaboration, indulgences, and various and sundry hijinks during the halcyon days of rock and roll excess.

Artist budgets are scaled to projected earnings (the more sales, the bigger the budgets). And in Rock and Roll Babylon, no one had compunctions about spending someone else's money: Fleetwood Mac's *Rumours* took a year to record and cost in excess of $1 million to make ($4.85 million in 2022 dollars), money that had to be recouped before the band saw a dime. (Fortunately for all concerned, *Rumours* sold 40 million units.) The Isleys were the antithesis of rock and roll hedonism: owning T-Neck meant managing their own money and time, and the group was loathe to waste either. Production was basic, with only their regular crew credited on the new project: the three older brothers, Ernie on guitars, drums, and percussion, Marvin on bass, Chris on keys, George Moreland on drums, Truman Thomas on organ, and Rocky on percussion—just a rhythm section, no horns or strings. Ernie, Marvin, and Chris demoed all the songs on four tracks in the Englewood family basement. "We're more conscious of recording costs and time," said Ernie. "We're not set to one formula and we don't spend hours sitting around and mixing and recording. We've gotten more discipline."[8]

The only outside input for the project—the entire reason for the LA relocation, in fact—was the production consultants the Isleys chose as collaborators, engineers Malcolm Cecil and Robert Margouleff. Cecil, a bassist/engineer on London's live music scene in the mid-1960s, and Margouleff, a collaborator with inventor Robert Moog and musician-on-call for Andy Warhol's Factory collective, bonded in New York over synths, and built The Original New Timbral Orchestra, or TONTO. It was the world's first and largest multitimbral polyphonic analog synthesizer, and seismically realigned pop music's sonic palette. They recorded a 1971 cult classic, *Zero Time*, under the name TONTO's Expanding Head Band. TONTO made them one of the most sought-after teams in the business, with devotees such as Weather Report, The Doobie Brothers, Billy Preston, Randy Newman, Quincy Jones, Stephen Stills, Gil Scott-Heron & Brian Jackson, Harry Nilsson, and Joan Baez—and, of course, Stevie Wonder, sui generis genius, who put TONTO on the map single-handed.

Wonder produced arguably the most creatively ambitious body of work in all of modern pop, and TONTO provided the tapestry for the bulk of that run—*Music of My Mind*, *Talking Book*, *Innervisions*, and *Fulfillingness' First Finale*. Wonder and TONTO had been at the Record Plant so often that Studio B was specifically designed for him and the duo to work there. The relationship formed when Wonder turned 21 and his contract at Motown was up. He sought creative control of his career, rather than being "handled" by the label. He moved to New York to immerse himself in the scene, and a copy of *Zero Time* landed in his hands. Imagining its possibilities, Wonder showed up on Cecil's doorstep. "[The Moog] is a way to directly express what comes from your mind. It gives you so much of a sound in the broader sense. What you're actually doing with an oscillator is taking a sound and shaping it into whatever form you want."[9]

The maturity and sonic expansion—not to mention the chart domination—of their former Tamla labelmate caught the

Isleys' attention. "Stevie Wonder was a big influence of mine," Jasper said. "When I heard the '*Music of My Mind*' album, it blew my mind. He used [synthesizer] in a different way than anyone ever thought of."[10] Cecil and Margouleff booked the Isleys to overlap sessions for *Innervisions*. The family hung out while Wonder was recording "Don't You Worry 'Bout a Thing." Ernie mused, "Imagine hearing [that] over and over. Man, that wasn't 'My Cherie Amour' or 'Superstition.' That made us think about what we were doing."[11]

However, this would be one of the rare indulgences the Isleys allowed. In sharp contrast to Wonder's freewheeling and experimentative approach, the family came in with their music methodically laid out, and once the red lights went on, all noses were pressed to the grindstone. Aside from coming up with sounds for TONTO and Ernie's guitars, Cecil and Margouleff mostly ran tape and mixed. "Working with The Isleys was much more business-like than working with Stevie," Margouleff said. "With Stevie, it was like living inside this world. We were part of every aspect of the creative process: shaping the songs and getting the sounds. We were much more on the outside of The Isley Brothers' trip. They were a very close-knit family, and we were like hired guns."[12]

According to the duo, The Isley Brothers were old school. O'Kelly handled all business matters and managed the money; Ronald was the interlocutor; and Rudolph was sergeant-at-arms, with his pistol close to handle whatever situations needed to be "handled." Margouleff remarked,

After one of the albums we worked on, O'Kelly and Marvin came into our office with a briefcase. They opened it up and there were hundreds of dollars, neatly stacked. Like something out of James Bond! They said, "How much do we owe you?" It was something like $20,000 to do the job, and they paid us in cash. It was the one and only time I've ever been paid like that.[13]

One significant shift with the new project was that Ernie, Marvin, and Chris—who were already in the touring band—were now also writing all the original material and crafting song arrangements, with the older brothers having the final say. This process began on *Givin' It Back* and evolved with each new release. As such, the decision—long time in coming—was made to finally introduce the revamped lineup. Hence the title of the first T-Neck/Epic release: *The Isley Brothers: 3+3*.

The approach to the new album continued the combination of established rock and pop interpretations with solid originals. Only now, after years of refinement, hit records, and dogged touring, the group was far more polished in the art of songcraft. They had four new originals, "If You Were There," "You Walk Your Way," "What It Comes Down To," and "Highways of My Life." Covers included James Taylor's "Don't Let Me Be Lonely Tonight," The Doobie Brothers' "Listen To The Music," Jonathan Edwards' "Sunshine (Go Away Today)," and Seals & Crofts' "Summer Breeze." However, one "cover" on the album, the most unexpected for the Isleys to reexamine, became the most impactful statement of their career.

Back in 1964 when the Isleys were on United Artists and collaborating with "Twist and Shout" cohort, Bert Berns, they brought in an original piece titled "Who's That Lady," a slinky mambo soul ballad inspired by The Impressions. It was one of the stronger efforts of the Isleys/Berns partnership, but the single went nowhere. Ronald is credited for digging this song out of the crates, but once "The Plus Three" contingent got their hands on it, they rebuilt an entirely different beast. Ernie and Chris wrote new lyrics, adding a driving rhythm, rocking piano, understated organ, and Ernie's signature rhythm and lead guitar parts over the top. And while previous outings alluded to The Isleys/Jimi Hendrix connection, 3+3 dove all the way in: Cecil was a childhood friend of Roger Mayer, the guitar tech who modified Hendrix's axes and built his effects pedals. Mayer took Ernie's Stratocaster and tweaked it to Hendrix's specifications and built an Octavia box, the juice behind Hendrix's signature wail. "We essentially Jimi Hendrix-ized Ernie when he was [21]. He was so blown away and enamored with it. He took to it like a duck to water."[14] On ballads, Ernie also overlaid ornate acoustic parts—on some pieces, using a twelve-string—which expanded the group's sonic palette. "I bought a 12-string from Manny's Music [in NYC]," he said. "We were looking for a different kind of feel. I tuned it up, started playing and got inspired."[15]

Indeed, when cutting the famous solo to "That Lady," Ernie was so deeply engaged—he played in the dark facing the wall so he couldn't see his brothers' giddy reactions—he wasn't aware he was tracking. It was the first of only two takes, and while he preferred the second, the first was chosen for vocal quality. "Everything went from black & white to technicolor," Ernie recalled. "I felt like I had one foot on the ground and the other on Mount Olympus, like I learned how to ride a bike and eat ice cream at the same time. [O']Kelly looked at me for 15 minutes straight without blinking."[16] Ernie added flourishes on "What It Comes Down To" and "Sunshine (Go Away Today)," but the only other true guitar showcase was "Summer Breeze," cranked up as a full-on rock ballad, closing out with a celestial solo driving the track into the fade.

Chris Jasper's keyboards were yin to Ernie's guitar yang, providing rhythm, color, and texture with piano and Rhodes, and funky countermelody on clavinet. The clavinet would feature more heavily in later outings, but gets a workout on "If You Were There," and "Listen to the Music," and is featured specifically on "Sunshine (Go Away Today)," as well as an exotic, middle-Eastern style synth melody (played in call-and-response to a guitar figure by Ernie). His most expressive use of TONTO is the closing gem, "Highways of My Life," opening with an extended piano figure that accentuated his classical background ("Most people didn't know they were getting a taste of Ravel and Debussy in with their funk," Jasper joked[17]). He sets a melancholy tone with a Wonder-esque melody winding through the head of each verse.

Truman Thomas' emotive organ, featured on half the album, grounds these songs in the Isleys' church background, most pronounced in the original, "You Walk Your Way," and a brief, uplifting solo in the breakdown of "That Lady." Marvin's fluid but sturdy, economic bass girds all the songs over George Moreland's expressive drum kit and Rocky's kinetic percussion. The band is locked tight, yet nimble and expressive. Remarkably, nearly all the music was tracked in one or two takes.

The Isleys always projected as a tight-knit unit, and it was imperative for Cecil and Margouleff to capture that feeling in the recordings. "What Malcolm and I brought was a sense of intimacy in terms of putting the musicians in the same room as the listener. We wanted it to sound very close. The instruments were all very tightly recorded. Not a lot of reverbs or effects,"[18] said Margouleff. Cecil added, "I had what I called the 'ducking limiter,' which was actually two stereo limiters. It was a way to ensure the vocals always cut through, no matter what was there underneath it."[19]

The whole album was cut in a brisk, intense three weeks. Margouleff said.

> There was never any hanging around. . . . Stevie would write in the studio, feeling his way. The Isleys came in prepared, knowing exactly what they wanted. They were a hard-working, industrious group, no drugs or alcohol, nothing like that. When they said they'd be in the studio at 10 in the morning, they'd be there exactly at 10. If somebody wasn't ready, they suffered the wrath of the other brothers. They ran a tight ship.[20]

The Isley Brothers: 3+3, despite its extensive preparation and strict execution, captured the full essence and creative energy of the live touring band, still feeling fresh and loose. The Isleys forged a distinct sound, blended from equal parts rock, soul, funk, and pop, with a touch of blues and classical, songs elevated above anything they'd ever done. Their T-Neck/Epic debut was the group's most cohesive creative statement to date.

It could have all been for naught. Clive Davis, the Isleys' benefactor, was unceremoniously fired from CBS on May

29, 1973. Arthur Taylor, CBS president and Davis' nemesis, leveled allegations of over \$94,000 in misappropriated corporate funds—including \$53,700 for apartment renovations and \$20,000 for his son's bar mitzvah. Davis was also accused of fostering a culture of payola within the company, taking \$6,500 cash from an in-house marketing VP.[21] He further faced a federal grand jury probe into interstate heroin trafficking and connections to payola-by-drugs. There were lower-tiered bad actors at Columbia, and Davis himself testified and confirmed payola within the company (payola is common among labels and was never illegal; only non-reporting of its practice and revenues is illegal). But the charges were strongly discredited and dismissed.[22] It is suspected that Davis' termination stemmed from CBS ass-covering ahead of a pending FCC payola investigation that threatened their broadcast licenses—considering all the success he delivered, Davis could have just returned the alleged "misappropriated funds." Regardless, he'd rise from the ashes to launch Arista Records in 1974, reclaiming (and expanding) his legend.

Fortunately, Ron Alexenberg, the newly appointed VP of A&R for Epic and Davis' right hand, picked things up. The album rollout was a major event: in June, CBS dropped a full-page ad in *Billboard* with the *3+3* album cover shot under the title "Meet That Lady": "Remember when The Isley Brothers launched their T-Neck record label with 'It's Your Thing,' one of the most influential records of all time? Now we welcome their new association with Columbia Records in a similar way: 'That Lady.' Another innovative new sound from the always brilliant Isley Brothers."[23] The company took out other ads in magazines and trades. What's key is they name *Columbia, not Epic* as the distributor—for the Isleys to have that cosign, when the company still wasn't all-in for Black music yet, was a huge deal.

The reception to "That Lady" was explosive: #2 on *Billboard* R&B, #6 on both *Cashbox* Top 100 and *Billboard* Hot 100, staying on the charts for nine weeks, ending the year at #21 on *Billboard's* Top 100. *3+3* was reviewed excitedly: Robert Christgau of *The Village Voice* declared it the group's "sexiest music in years";[24] Tony Cummings of *Black Music* extolled "the genuine article, a quite stupendous fusion of everything the Isleys have been into over the years";[25] Vernon Gibbs of *Essence* praised, "With six people creating as one, feeding on the harmony that exists between them as brothers, musicians, and businessmen, they have crafted an infinite set of possibilities."[26]

The album's arrival on August 7 was as plain-spoken and bold as its lead single: against a backdrop of stark black, not three, but *six* Isleys, adorned in riveting silk, leather, and denim suits, Ernie and Marvin each brandishing their guitars. The album opened to a gatefold introducing all the members individually against a white backdrop, left to right: Ronald, O'Kelly, Rudolph, Ernie, Chris, and Marvin. Again, as they have on all of their fencepost releases, all stared intently, proudly, *defiantly*, into the camera. Again, subtext—unmistakable: "You have never seen brothers (hereditary and/or cultural) like this before. *And now* there are *six* of us. *Plus, now* we're a *band*. Deal with *that*." The two follow-up singles, "What It Comes Down To" (#5 R&B, #55 Hot 100) and "Summer Breeze" (#10 R&B, #60 Hot 100), each fared better in urban formats than crossover, but still represented the best overall showing since *It's Our Thing*. It finished the year at #2 on the *Billboard* Black Albums chart (only behind, not surprisingly, Stevie Wonder's *Innervisions*) and #8 on the US *Billboard* Pop Albums chart. *The Isley Brothers 3+3* was a rare triumph of a Black artist crossing multiple radio formats: urban, Top 40, MOR, progressive rock, and even a few AOR stations. Most importantly, the album shipped double platinum, the first Isleys' album ever to do so.

The Isley Brothers 3+3's release was part of a banner year (1973) for career-defining albums across the board. Ruefully, albums by Black acts were mostly overlooked—irrespective of mastery—as conventional wisdom dictated Black pop only had viability through singles. This severely hampered these artists' ability to maximize audience reach. *3+3*, along with *Innervisions* (Stevie Wonder), *Fresh* (Sly & The Family Stone), *Hey Now Hey (The Other Side of the Sky)* (Aretha Franklin), *Headhunters* (Herbie Hancock), *Extension of a Man* (Donny Hathaway), and *Head to the Sky* (Earth Wind & Fire), sold comparably to White rock albums (several have resurfaced on "Best Albums of the 1970s" lists by *Rolling Stone*, *Pitchfork*, and *Paste*). Still, these works got no such notice from the rock establishment as albums like *Dark Side of the Moon* (Pink Floyd), *Quadrophenia* (The Who), *Goodbye Yellow Brick Road* (Elton John), *Aladdin Sane* (David Bowie), *Houses of the Holy* (Led Zeppelin), and *Greetings from Asbury Park* (Bruce Springsteen). What set the Isleys apart was the intentional reclamation of their rock and roll space only fifteen years after once being in the epicenter of all rock was about, even influencing top White artists who followed their footsteps.

Owning the label gave the Isleys leverage to make creative and commercial choices thought "counterintuitive" for marketing Black artists. But with their track record of lulls after success, how long could the high of *The Isley Brothers 3+3* last?

4
Fight the Power
The Isleys' Classic Run and the Battle for Crossover Success

The progressive/freeform radio formats that were the primary conduits for rock music began dying off by the early 1970s, giving way to tightened playlists, focused and succinct jocks, and regular commercial intervals. This translated into consistent target audience delivery and profits.[1] Celebrated programmers and consultants Lee Abrams and Kent Burkhart are cited as refining and codifying the modern album-oriented rock (AOR) format that exists currently.[2] AOR dominated radio due to its staunch following of 18- to 34-year-old White males, generating up to $4 million per added ratings point in ad dollars per year. Its "widespread acceptance by the industry as an official format marked the complete standardization of commercial FM rock."[3]

Format radio brought a windfall, but many have argued it also genericized the airwaves through (a) a reduction of music's sonic and cultural palette; (b) a glacial pace to breaking new acts and styles; (c) pandering demo-driven jock interplay; (d) pervasive influence of record companies, consultants, and promoters/payola; and (e) and growing intrusion of commercials.[4] These trends became more prevalent through consolidation, cloned signals, and syndicated programs. The slightest variety fractured audiences (rock stations juggling AOR, MOR, prog rock, punk, new wave, etc.; urban stations juggling soul, electro-funk, hip-hop, and pop). In AOR specifically, Kim Simpson, author of the survey *Early 70s Radio: The American Format Revolution*, notes, "The more tightly formatted FM rock became, the more inflexible its audience seemed to be."[5]

For The Isley Brothers—and other artists of color, women, LGTBQIA, and other non-White/male/binary groups—the openness of progressive radio gave access to loyal rock fans. AOR shut them out. Urban radio was equally inflexible but actually played more White rock artists than AOR did Black rock artists: Elton John, Queen, David Bowie, The Eagles, Boz Scaggs, Blondie, Hall & Oates, Toto, Steely Dan, and others crossed singles over to Black listeners with great success. The Rolling Stones' "Miss You" got more spins on Black radio than any Jimi Hendrix single ever did.[6]

Compounding matters, a nascent (White) rock intelligentsia—media, producers, journalists, critics, promoters, and emergent academics—advanced the contrivance that Black performers "didn't belong" in rock music.[7] The rock press assaulted Black pop as "repetitive," "juvenile," "inauthentic," "commercial"—insinuating inferiority of Black pop to White rock music.[8] This conceit is encapsulated in one 1973 commentary:

> For a long time, like most White kids, I had very little use for Black music; I liked Hendrix, of course I dug the

blues, and later on I got to know and love Miles Davis and all the other jazzmen, but the bulk of Black music made me turn a paler shade of white [*sic*]. It seemed so slick, contrived and phony, not "real" music at all, just commercial confection of about the same aesthetic level of The Archies.[9]

Vainglorious White critics and other gatecrashers-turned-gatekeepers inseminated themselves as authority over a culture completely alien to them less than two decades prior and fabricated standards to disqualify the form's Black practitioners, as if these newcomers were sole arbiters on "quality" or "authenticity," or as if none of these gripes applied equally to their White rock idols, or as if the value Black people placed on their own music carried no worth. This condescension reflected and amplified the mindset of ill-informed (and, at times, outright bigoted) White rock fans. Format radio muddled identity politics and quality/style, stifling Black creative freedom and earning power.[10]

And while urban radio kept the Isleys in the public eye, economic structures suppressed the value of Black media, artists, and music. Urban trailed "general market" formats in earnings, as ad buyers engaged bias-driven practices behind closed doors—demanding lower ad rates, limiting or skipping urban buys due to "income thresholds" or "negative research data." Urbans in top markets can deliver top five ratings yet only bill at a rate of 71 percent of general market stations, even those sub-Top 20. These procedures were verified in a December 1998 report commissioned by the FCC.[11] In 1979, an assistant station manager groused to *Radio & Records*:

One thing Black stations should understand is that their advertisers don't want to be there. If an advertiser could, he'd want to be on the number one, two or three radio stations in the market. They don't trust it, they don't understand it, they still don't believe that Black people in this day and age control billions of dollars in this country.[12]

The Isley Brothers battled through this environment for the next few years as they embarked on the most successful run of their career. Starting with *3+3*, they assembled a streak of million-selling albums—some even garnered support from a few AOR stations—but mostly facing resistance from the rock music establishment.

Live It Up, 1974 (RIAA Certified Platinum—1,000,000 sales)

The summer of 1974 was fraught with several national calamities, most notably President Richard M. Nixon resigning in disgrace for his role in the break-in of the Democratic National Committee HQ and its ham-fisted cover-up. It was symbolic of the dissatisfaction and unrest gripping the country. Segregated radio deterred disparate music communities from converging (although Top 40 made a valiant effort), but allowed each to satiate within their own respective corners. The Isleys welcomed anyone who cared to listen, "We became known as 'the summer group,'" said Marvin. "Every summer we were going to have a hot album out, and it was like, 'Look forward to the summer as the Isley Brothers time of year.'"[13]

The group returned to LA to work at the Record Plant with Malcolm Cecil and Robert Margouleff—the two just completed Stevie Wonder's latest masterpiece, *Fulfillingness' First Finale*, and were collaborating on Minnie Riperton's Epic debut, *Perfect Angel*. The group streamlined even further, focused on originals (the only cover is Todd Rundgren's classic "Hello, It's Me"). The younger Isleys did nearly all of the instrumentation: George Moreland (drums), Karl Potter (percussion), and Truman Thomas (organ) are credited, but they're featured only on three pieces: "Brown-Eyed Girl," a plaintive, soulful ballad with folk overtones, enhanced by lush twelve-string guitar, sweeping acoustic piano, and the brothers delivering one of their most sophisticated vocal arrangements; Chris' mournful "Lovers Eve," highlighting his majestic piano and emotive synthesizers in union with Ronald's wrought and lovelorn vocal; and the blues ballad, "Ain't I Been Good To You (Part 1 & 2)" (an idea from Marvin, it morphs from a funk hump to a slow waltz, highlighting Ernie's searing guitar).

As to the album's starting point, "Live It Up" is introduced by Ernie in the drum chair (he would take over on drums on subsequent records), delivering his signature straight four-to-the-floor pulse, a weaving call-and-response bass part by Marvin, and a driving Rhodes electric piano by Chris with funk confetti from a clavinet sprinkled over the top. Ron sneaks in half groan/half growl and builds to the release of the chorus, where the brothers chant the song title and, finally, taken to climax by Ernie's economic, but still fiery, solo work. "Need a Little Taste of Love" is a quick, cheerful confection with a generous sampling of Ernie soloing throughout. "Midnight Sky" revisits some of the musical themes of "That Lady"—a few references to the former song are sprinkled in—again, striking the fine balance between Ronald as balladeer and rocker. And the brothers' take on "Hello, It's Me" transforms Rundgren's pop whimsy into a subdued bedroom confessional, full of melancholy and waning optimism channeled through Ronald's emotionally weary vocal. The song became a classic in late-night "Quiet Storm" segments on urban/Black radio formats.

All six brothers confidently stood on the *Live It Up* front cover in resplendent garb, while on the back were individual shots underneath their names, birthdates, and zodiac signs (the de rigueur among Black folks in the 1970s), and the inside sleeve provided lyrics. It was the first album the brothers gave credit to Mother Sallye Bernice (this became a ritual on all Isley albums going forward). *Live* was released in September with another full-court press in ads and promotion, including billboards in urban markets. And the outcome was similar: *Live It Up* vaulted to #1 on *Billboard* Soul Albums and #14 Pop Albums. The title single reached #4 R&B and #52 Pop. The second release, "Midnight Sky," reached #8 R&B and #73 Pop. The album shipped platinum—the first time the Isleys went platinum back-to-back. Extensive touring followed—as headliners and co-bills—as well as TV dates, like *Soul Train*, *Don Kirshner's Rock Concert*, and *Midnight Special*.

While the album did extremely well, the gap between audiences widened, with urban sales outperforming crossover pop sales, despite high sales overall. *Live It Up* built its strengths on an album-driven formula without any album-based platform to boost it. The suspicion was, with the growing dominance of AOR formats, the album didn't get the support the band felt it deserved. "We still encounter pockets of resistance to our music amongst radio stations in this country, just like everyone else," said Ernie, "There's no one group who gets automatic and immediate response from R&B and pop markets on every release—you still have to break through."[14]

The Heat Is On, 1975 (RIAA Certified Double Platinum—2,000,000 sales)

The year 1975 was fraught with national angst: the Vietnam Conflict ended disastrously; major cities defaulted (most famously New York City); unemployment neared 10 percent. Still, another summer on the horizon, the Isleys got busy on a new album—only now, Ernie, Chris, and Marvin would be *entirely* responsible for every note. Ernie, who played half the instruments, mused, "In the studio, I didn't get a break. I didn't sit back and have a chocolate malt and a burger. I'd get back out there and play."[15] Cecil and Margouleff also returned, but with no Stevie Wonder project—they split over royalties and credit disputes. They relocated to Kendun Recorders in Burbank, while Wonder toiled at Record Plant on his magnum opus, *Songs in the Key of Life*.

Songs for the new album, *The Heat Is On*, came just as the work for *Live It Up* completed. The whole family—Mother

Sallye, wives, and kids—were in Los Angeles while the brothers worked. Once the album was done, the family had a day planned at Disneyland. Ernie was in the shower and lyrics came: "Time is truly wasting / There's no guarantee / Smile is in the making / We got to fight the powers that be . . ."[16] The idea was so compelling that the guitarist jumped out mid-shower. "Soap went this way, shower curtain went that way, looking for a pencil to write it down," recounts Ernie. "Had that in my hip pocket, but I didn't say anything about it until two or three months later."[17] It wasn't even the first song to be recorded—that fell to the title track. Two pieces were cut the same day: the shower piece, titled "Fight the Power," and "Harvest for the World," the former chosen for the new album, and the latter held for the next.

"Fight" had a signature Isley groove; however, Ronald exercised executive privilege with the lyric. As written, the bridge section went: "I try to play my music, they say the music's too loud / I try talkin' about it, I got the big runaround / And when I rolled with the punches, I got knocked to the ground / By all the *nonsense* goin' down."[18] Ronald opted for something with a lot more scat—the indelible (and now immortal) "BULLSHIT." Ernie admitted to being stunned. "I said, 'Some people may not like it.' [Ronald] said, 'Ernie, if you can say what you feel, and it's embraced, wonderful. If you can say what you feel, and it's not embraced, *at least you said what you feel.*'[19]" (Mother Sallye Bernice did voice her displeasure with her church-reared boys cursing.)

"Fight the Power" was embraced—whether for the groove, the message, or just the impish glee of such a coarse word in the middle of a pop record (a "clean" version was edited for radio). Released May 31, 1975, it was the lead single for *The Heat Is On* album and was the song of the summer, in all formats. It hit #4 on *Billboard* Hot 100, #1 on *Billboard* R&B, #13 on *Billboard* Dance/Disco, and #6 on *Cash Box* Top 100. It ranked #27 in the year-end *Billboard* charts and the album sold double platinum.

The Heat Is On wasn't a "concept album," but it was constructed as one: up-tempo songs on side A, ballads on side B, each clocking in over five minutes, but only six total pieces and a complete time of thirty-seven minutes. The idea was quite simple—to allow each side of the record to play uninterrupted. "People would be dancing to one of our fast numbers," Ernie explained, "and then, just as soon as they were really gettin' into it, a slow tune would crop up and stop the action."[20]

The title piece was written by Chris, with a clavinet-heavy hook and bass synth hump squatting on a mid-tempo groove by Ernie and Marvin—it features the first of only two guitar solos on the record (it was actually cut twice, as the drums and mics were incorrectly set up on the initial take). "Hope You Feel Better Love" is an up-tempo Jekyll/Hyde tune that glides between sweet and mournful, kept aloft by strumming rhythm guitar, and then flipping to a raucous rock bridge in a modulated key, before surrendering to another devastating solo by Ernie trailing out to the end.

The ballad side opens with the classic "For the Love of You," a breezy piece featuring lush acoustic guitars and creamy keyboard layers. It almost didn't make the album—in fact, it threatened the album's release entirely. The song, originally titled, "How Lucky I Am," was written by Rudolph for his wife, Elaine. However, Ernie, Chris, and Marvin completely reworked the song, and Rudolph reportedly didn't take kindly to the change. He fumed, "That ain't my song! That ain't *nothin!*'" and attempted to block the album release until his song was reinstated. Only the threat of delaying their million-dollar advance quelled him,[21] which, in the end, proved fortunate: "For the Love of You" landed #10 on *Billboard* R&B and #22 on *Billboard* Hot 100, the first time the Isleys had two Top 40 hits from the same album since 1972's *Brother, Brother, Brother*. "Living" was followed by another lush piece by Chris, "Sensuality," an intimate slow song with a complex chord progression and rich synths. The final track, "Make Me Say It Again Girl," is an Ernie piece built around blended acoustic guitars and synths.

On the subject of radio, the Isleys weren't overtly political by any stretch, and "Fight the Power" didn't decry any specific grievance—"A lot of people thought we were talking about the Black situation," Marvin said, "but the song wasn't about any one situation. It was just talking about whatever the powers are that be. Because a lot of different things have power over different people."[22] But the song was interpreted (rightly or wrongly) as a loose broadside against the rock music establishment. "We thought it was jive basically," Ernie said laughing. "We just put it in their face anyway."[23]

Such misinterpretation was justified. The band had three straight million-plus-selling LPs that weren't recognized by rock radio and media. Cliff White, a critic for *New Music Express*, called out rock critics: "The Isley Brothers are currently on the critical chopping block," he wrote, "out of favour [*sic*] with a lot of white writers (not so with black

American record buyers) for failing to match their 'That Lady' single and *3+3* album on one hand, and repeating themselves on the other. It seems critics' confusion only really became acute when albums usurped singles in the industry's affection."[24]

Harvest for the World, 1976 (RIAA Certified Platinum—1,000,000 sales)

America's Bicentennial was celebrated with great pomp and circumstance, but discontent was a huge part of society's undercurrent. A complete outsider, Democrat James Earl Carter, former governor of Georgia, came from nowhere to topple establishment Republican Gerald R. Ford and was elected the president of the United States. With a nation preparing to celebrate its 200th birthday that summer, the Isleys were intent on having their music at parties nationwide.

The band was back at the Record Plant—it'd be the last album they'd cut with Cecil and Margouleff. But only Cecil was available to engineer and program TONTO for the new album, *Harvest for the World*. The title track came from Ernie messing around on his twelve-string guitar at the Englewood home. The title referenced a line from the Gospel of Matthew: "Send labourers into the Lord's harvest." Ronald recalled, "The song had super meaning, which was inspiring as a vocalist, because you want to deliver the message as best you can."[25] Cecil recalled, "My main thrust was to get people from Stevie Wonder on to do socially conscious songs. So 'Harvest' was gratifying to me. I felt that we had a big opportunity to reach people through the music."[26]

A prelude using motifs from "Let Me Down Easy" and "People of Today" was created to introduce the piece. Chris explained, "I remember saying, 'This is a great message here. It'd be nice if there was a set up. So 'Harvest For The World (Prelude),' was done on the spot in the studio."[27] The song upshifts to a mellow groove, adorned by lush piano and crystalline acoustic guitars. Ronald's soulful plea for compassion—"All babies together, every one a seed / Half of us are satisfied, half of us in need / Love's bountiful in us, tarnished by our greed / Oh, when will there be a harvest for the world"[28]—subdued until the end, erupts with a preacher's intensity and all the brothers vamp the chorus. "Harvest" landed at #9 on *Billboard* R&B and #63 on *Billboard* Hot 100.

"People of Today," a funk rock groove driven by clavinet and a machine gun staccato guitar line, is a Chris song that takes society's temperature in a general, slice-of-life manner, layered with keys and vocoder. It charted at #3 on *Billboard* dance but nowhere else. "Who Loves You Better," the only rock guitar feature on the album, revisits some of the same musical territory as "Hope You Feel Better Love." This was the first single released from the album, scoring #2 on *Billboard* dance, #3 on *Billboard* R&B, and #47 pop, just barely missing another Top 40 trifecta. "(At Your Best) You Are Love," another mellow ballad layered with acoustic guitars and thick Rhodes, wasn't released as a single but became another Quiet Storm staple.

Filling out the album were bedroom dream "Let Me Down Easy," a ballad marrying Ernie's acoustic and Chris' synths; "So You Wanna Stay Down," a brisk, danceable trifle with layered acoustic guitars driving the groove; and "Feel the Need," the album closer (perhaps the record's sleeper track), a slow funk grind, with a deep rhythm pocket, punchy clavinet, and a surgical rhythm guitar. Ronald's vocals dominated, the brothers only providing backing on three of the album's eight tracks.

Harvest for the World dropped on May 29, 1976, to positive reviews and strong support, but wasn't the juggernaut that *The Heat Is On* and *3+3* were. Still, while *Harvest* didn't have the firepower of past releases, the album as a whole continued the Isleys' streak of million sellers. The group conceded disappointment with the mixes and lack of heat. "When you play the acoustic stuff, you tend to get a certain sound," Ernie reasoned. "*Harvest for the World* is a platinum album, and without a gold single on it. Overall, some of the things we tried to do at home didn't come out with as much fire in the studio as they should have. That happens sometimes."[29]

Go for Your Guns, 1977 (RIAA Certified Double Platinum—2,000,000 sales)

The Isleys were determined to have that watershed LP to firmly put them on top and decided to shake things up. For starters, the LA trips became draining, time-consuming, and costly. Chris discovered Bearsville Studios in Woodstock, NY, and drove up to investigate. Founded by Albert Grossman, former manager for Bob Dylan, Bearsville is a world-class recording complex two hours north of New York

City, outfitted with two studios, performance theater, remote recording facilities, artist apartments, restaurants, and lush natural surroundings. Grossman discovered the spot in 1964, with the goal of building an artist-friendly haven away from the hassles of most big city facilities. Luminaries such as Todd Rundgren, NRBQ, Carla Bley, Meat Loaf, The Band, Taj Mahal, The Butterfield Blues Band, Foghat, The Rolling Stones, Janis Joplin, Rush, Patti Smith, R.E.M., and others recorded pinnacle albums here. "The studio had basically the same set-up as California," Chris said. "I said, 'Hey, guys, instead of going 3,000 miles, we can go maybe a hundred miles upstate and get the same sound.'"[30]

Work started in November of 1976. Bearsville's noted in-house engineers John Holbrook and Tom Mark were tapped to work the console while the Isleys supervised. The brothers chose to dig deeper into harder rock and funk sounds, hence the title *Go for Your Guns*. "We wanted to be more aggressive," said Ernie.[31] All the songs had swagger and edge, and each groove leaned into with purpose and drive—even the ballads. The band was tighter, the energy higher, and the mixes cleaner while retaining ferocity and rawness. "We were closer to home," Ernie said. "The atmosphere was more relaxed and we noticed a certain freshness as a result."[32]

The lead single, "The Pride," starts the album off, a percussive funk groove with churning drums and bass, chopping clavinet, accenting Rhodes piano, and a popping call-and-response guitar figure. It relents to a bridge with layered Rhodes and Ronald weaving with the group's rich harmonies: "Don't you think it's *fascinating* . . . ?" Turning around to the chorus, Ronald urges, "It's the pride / That you fee-ee-eel / It's the pride." The brothers whisper in response, "When you finally break it on down, it's the pride."[33] The lyric is a reminder to politicos of their obligations to the public that empowers them.

Following "Pride" is "Footsteps in the Dark," an anguished ballad about the uncertainty of love and the ambivalence it can manifest. The song is bass and drums forward, with layered guitars over lush keyboards and clavinet accents. Instruments fall away as Ronald painfully wails, "Are we really sure / Can a love that's lasted for so long still endure / Do I really care / Hey, let's talk about the distractions goin' on elsewhere . . ."[34] Wrapping up the first side is "Tell Me When You Need It Again," which stomps along with all the brothers crying out the chorus with a lead rock guitar melody from Ernie. Isley percussionist Everett Collins is credited on congas for this track.

Side two is a rock tour de force, starting with "Climbin' Up the Ladder," a blistering anthem as legitimate as anything on AOR radio. The piece is built around a twinned guitar and bass line and clavinet doubling with power chords as a foundation for Ernie's versatility, flipping between chugging rhythm and shredding solos (this piece features three). Ronald roars out a testimony to remaining true to one's convictions despite adversity. "Voyage To Atlantis" is the Isleys' take on the classic sailor rock ballad, where a shipman pines for his distant lover while away at sea. Heavy flanges and phasers give the guitars and keys the effect of water and Ernie's guitar lines cry with the ache of longing, while Ronald and the brothers sing almost in prayer, "I'll always/Come back to you . . ."[35] The final suite is an electrified rock/funk number contributed by Marvin, called "Livin' in the Life," which decries outsiders' distorted views of fame. The band pounds on an up-tempo groove with weaving guitar, keys, and bass. Ronald snarls at all the sycophants and haters: "And if you think it's easy / It's only 'cause you ain't me / And I ain't you / Check out the difference between the two . . ."[36] After a false stop, the band launches back into the groove—now the instrumental title track—and Ernie blazes again to the fade.

Go for Your Guns blew the doors off on April 16, 1977, peaking a month later at #1 on *Billboard* Soul Albums and #6 on *Billboard* Pop Albums. The album spawned three singles: "The Pride" (#1 R&B, #63 Pop), "Livin' in the Life" (#4 R&B, #40 Pop), and "Voyage to Atlantis" (#50 R&B). "Footsteps in the Dark" was never officially a single, but, again, ended up being a huge hit on Quiet Storm segments. The album stayed on the charts for forty weeks, finishing the year double platinum with over two million copies sold. According to Ernie, *Go for Your Guns* was "our biggest album to date."[37]

But no one would know listening to AOR radio, reading top rock publications, following the top rock tours, or anywhere within the rock establishment's ecosystem. "It's true that we've managed to build up a solid crossover audience, but we want acceptance on everybody's part," Ernie said. "It can be done but it takes time—you just keep adding new people with every new release, hopefully."[38] An altruistic sentiment, but the Isleys were now officially twenty years in the business, bringing to mind a James Baldwin quote: "How much time do you want for your 'progress?'"

5
Showdown
Crossover Politics and the Battle against the AOR Cognoscenti

August 16, 1977, was a pivotal date in rock and roll history. Elvis Aaron Presley, much-celebrated installed rock monarch, died at Graceland, his Memphis, TN mansion, from cardiac arrest brought about by years of health issues and suspected drug and alcohol abuse. The Isleys never crossed paths with Presley, though they briefly shared the RCA label, the teams of Hugo & Luigi and Lieber & Stoller, and Wand's Florence Greenburg. Presley's death ended a twenty-year career teeming in triumph, controversy, and tragedy. It also severed ties to nearly all pre-Beatles Era rockers, confining them to "oldies but goodies," seen on "Happy Days," "American Graffiti," and PBS fundraisers.

Of greater significance was the erasure of the Black rock pioneers who preceded or were contemporaries to Presley (like The Isley Brothers). Chuck Berry, Little Richard, Fats Domino, Bo Diddley, Big Mama Thorton, and legions left this world with far less regard than Presley, though many still had more viable careers than his at the end. The Isleys, also twenty years in the business, were having the biggest hit streak of their career. But the rock establishment simply ignored them and all Black performers who made it possible for Presley and his acolytes to flourish. Case in point, the new Isleys' album, *Showdown*, released in April 1978, was another platinum seller, #1 *Billboard* R&B and #4 on *Billboard* Top 200, but no pop singles at all. Isley albums did crossover numbers, but weren't getting crossover airplay, exposure, nor money—and they were quite fed up about it.

The Isleys got to vent their frustrations through rock music's largest megaphone, *Rolling Stone*. (Ironically, the issue featured comic actor John Belushi, promoting the film "Animal House," with the frat party scene with fictional band Otis Day & The Knights performing the Isleys' "Shout," reviving sales for the song.) "There's no excuse," Ernie Isley fumed. He continued:

> If a person says, "We cannot play a particular artist because they have a particular sound," that's cool. But then you cut a song like "Summer Breeze," and they say, "I can't play that." You cut a song like "Fight The Power"—"I can't play that." You cut "Climbing Up The Ladder," "Livin' In The Life/Go For Your Guns,"—"I can't play that." Now, you're sayin', "Okay, what is it I have to put in the grooves for you to be able to play?" Then they say, "It's not a question of your sales. It's just a question of, we don't want to play it."[1]

O'Kelly Isley made it plain: "If you want to know why Fleetwood Mac and groups like Boston sell eight to ten million albums—they got a better shot at it. They're played constantly, once an hour and everywhere on 50,000-watt stations. That makes a difference. The more that people hear you, the more people buy your music." He stresses, "I don't think we would have any problem crossing over if the color of the skin were different. It's not the color of the music."[2]

The tagline on the contents page for the Isley piece reads: "Nineteen years after the success of 'Shout,' the Isleys are bitter about their exclusion from the 'Great White Marketplace.'"[3] "Bitter" is a tangled word, and one can no more read that into the Isleys' comments than one can read the intent behind the writer's or editor's inference. Ultimately, it's a cheap deflection: given their tenure and all they accomplished, they were *still deliberately refused a seat at rock's core table*—did the Isleys *not* have a legitimate point? If they were "bitter," didn't they have just cause to be?

In spite of its ore genesis to popular genres globally, Black music has historically matriculated into the American scene through a matrix of anti-Black bias and processes that inherently disadvantage its creators, stewards, and stakeholders. As ethnomusicologist Reebee Garafalo explains,

The history of popular music in this country can be described in terms of a pattern of Black innovation and White popularization. The pattern is built not only on the wellspring of creativity Black artists bring to popular music, but also the systematic exclusion of Black personnel from positions of power within the industry, and on the artificial separation of Black and White audiences. Because of industry and audience racism, Black music has been relegated to a separate and unequal marketing structure.

As a result, it is only on rare occasions that Black music "crosses over" into the mainstream on its own terms.[4]

The (White) rock intelligentsia crafted a unilateral narrative—"unilateral" insofar as no Black people were granted a rebuttal—of White "authority," "authenticity," and, by inference, "supremacy" in rock. Eric Weisbard unpacks these attitudes in *Top 40 Democracy: The Rival Mainstreams of American Music*:

> White critic Richard Corliss contrasted the "pop R&B exemplified by The Shirelles and The Isley Brothers" with "the visceral, dirt-pure stuff of John Lee Hooker and Bo Diddley." Taking Larry Neal in a decidedly new direction, a writer in *Sounds*, a progressive rock magazine, claimed, "Today's soul, the REAL music, not the 'sock-it-to-me,' or 'is everybody happy' corn, is being sung by Whites. 'Sock-it-to-me' Blacks, such as The Isleys, were replaced as figures of rebellion by the likes of Janis Joplin and Van Morrison." Keir Keightly concludes, "Raised on Top 40 and unafraid of popular success for select, *authentic* rock performers, the newborn rock culture featured a massive youth audience, which saw itself, nonetheless, as opposed to the mass mainstream and all that stood for."[5]

The prevailing modality among the AOR cognoscenti was to aggressively diminish and expunge Black presence and participation in the genre while conflating and amplifying its own *with absolutely no substantive nor objective criterion to base such a premise*. The blanket script was Black popular music "didn't fit the format," despite similar corollaries in heavy rotation by White rock artists (scant submissions by Black artists to AOR programmers are even vetted). The level of cognitive disconnect approaches Orwellian, culturally dissociating the dram-full of Black performers accepted in AOR. One director out of Kansas City was asked if his station played Black music: "It depends on what you consider. Stevie Wonder of course is not Black. And that's the kind of stuff we play and consider it Black. But we really don't, no."[6]

This isn't to say the Isleys didn't get any airplay on AOR stations at all—some stations fought to keep Black presence on the air. Weisbard cites John Gorman, program director at WMMS-FM in Cleveland, noting, "Incumbent album-rock stations were falling as new, tight-listed stations entered the market. . . . Wanting to avoid that, we had to take fewer liberties than we once could, while still breaking new music and taking a chance on a Labelle or Isley Brothers, moves that other album rock stations wouldn't make."[7] A rare Black AOR programmer, Bob Gooding at WCOL in Columbus, OH, fought against "the kind of programming in which we say, 'OK, we don't play any Black music other than Stevie Wonder.'"[8] But anti-Blackness overwhelmingly won out on rock radio: legendary New York jock, Bill "Rosko" Mercer, was fired from *two* stations that flipped to AOR—WNEW in 1967 and WKTU in 1985—despite being one of the founding fathers of the progressive rock format (WOR) and one of the most popular figures on-air. Outspoken on racism in AOR formats, Rosko said, "We must remove ourselves from the delusion that there's no racism in music. People are racist. And people make music. Therefore, there is racism in music."[9]

Exacerbating problems for non-White, non-male, non-cisgender/binary artists in the late 1970s was the rock establishment's apoplectic reaction to the explosion of popular dance music—the so-called "disco movement." Disco emerged from underground clubs in the 1960s in New York and Philadelphia by way of Detroit, attracting predominantly Black, LatinX, Italian, and LGTBQIA crowds, and served as safe scenes for complete identity and free expression.[10] But as it went mainstream in the 1970s, its popularity drew the ire of legions of rock devotees witnessing their corporeal and psychic dominance over the pop music landscape being threatened.

The vitriol aimed at the genre (and, indirectly, the people who engaged it) fueled a scorched-earth subculture war, fought largely in the media and over the air—often accompanied with gaslighting and half-hearted apologia—but at times escalating into real-world harm. Some AOR stations hosted disco destruction events—ironic, considering rock suffered similar campaigns in the 1950s. In a Portland drive-in screening of "Animal House," 900 patrons smashed records, chanting "Disco sucks!"[11]

The most flagrant manifestation was Disco Demolition Night, a promotional record burning at Chicago's Comiskey Park, July 12, 1979, that resulted in a full-on conflagration and on-field stampede by lathered-up rock fans. The field was destroyed and the White Sox were forced to forfeit the game and do extensive repairs. To date, the event organizer, jock Steve Dahl, insists there was never any malicious, racist, or homophobic intent or expression that night—just a bunch of rowdy kids who "got a bit out of hand." But a few Black attendees begged to differ: one usher pointed out White fans didn't bring just "disco" records, but Black records of *all* genres, many attendees breaking them in the face of any Black person available, bellowing "Disco sucks!" The event may not have actively targeted Black, LGTBQIA, LatinX, or women, but it pulled back the curtain on a lot of sublimated antagonism toward them.[12]

The "anti-disco backlash" shrank all crossover airplay and devastated sales for Black pop records. Singles by Black performers comprised one-third of pop hits since 1968, but precipitously shrank to one-twentieth by 1981.[13] The most sinister aspect of this campaign was Black acts who had *nothing whatsoever to do with the genre* suffered as well: the Isleys, Richie Havens, WAR, Shuggie Otis, Joan Armatrading, Labelle, Funkadelic, Billy Preston, Mother's Finest, Mandrill, and others defied stereotyping. Was their music played in discos? Of course, it was. As were records by The Rolling Stones, KISS, Rod Stewart, Queen, Electric Light Orchestra, and other White rock acts, none of whom lost cool points among the faithful.[14] Did the inclusion of these Black artists on disco playlists define them as disco acts like Donna Summer, The Village People, Cerrone, Meco, or Silver Convention? Not even faintly. "We're glad they play our records in the discos," O'Kelly said, "But we *hope* they'll play our records *everywhere*."[15] As cultural documentarian Nelson George noted in his influential book, *The Death of Rhythm and Blues*:

> As a cultural force, the term "disco" went out as quickly as it had come in. Unfortunately, all black dance music

was for a time labeled "disco." It was stupid. It was racist. It revealed again how important semantics can be in the reception of pop music. Just as rock and roll came to mean white music, disco came to represent some ugly amalgam of black and gay music.[16]

In the end, the *Rolling Stone* profile did nothing to even address the issues behind the band's complaints, never mind dissect or resolve them. The magazine certainly didn't look inward at the rock establishment and its cultural blind spots. While O'Kelly offered blanket optimism—"We'll let our music speak for us, and, some way, somehow, it'll open doors"—Ernie remained adamant: "I wouldn't be satisfied until we would be able to sell four to five million albums per release. What that's going to take is a single that sells 2.5 to three million units."[17]

In the meantime, *Showdown*, the second album the Isleys recorded at Bearsville, continued their million-selling album streak, irrespective of whatever rock stations thought. On the strength of the single "Take Me to the Next Phase," a deep, growling synth funk groove with a marching, military rhythm, the group topped the R&B charts again. As was customary, they also tugged heartstrings with the sweeping ballad "Groove with You," layered with Ernie's chord phrases and Chris' percussive Rhodes. An album track, "Coolin' Me Out," became a cruising anthem in car cultures, as well as Quiet Storm segments. Ernie's soloing would only appear on two pieces, the blues-funk of "Ain't Givin' Up No Love" and the energetic dance closer "Love Fever."

The tracks for *Showdown* had cleaner arrangements and crisper mixes, perhaps, in deference to the new styles, mastering, and compression technology that reshaped the sound of Black music heading into the 1980s. But the starkest departure was no polemics, no complex arrangements, no lofty aspirations—this album was pure escapism: just party and love songs. This would be the modus operandi for the Isleys (and Black pop in general) going forward. *Showdown* finished the year at #9 on the *Billboard* R&B album chart and #82 on *Billboard* Hot 100. The growing disparity between urban and pop charts also became a recurring theme.

The year 1979 was one of momentous shifts in Black music. The industry overall was in a recession: music sales fell 26.4 percent between 1977 and 1980, with the "anti-disco backlash" dragging Black sales even further.[18] While there were cost reductions across the board, Black music divisions took the brunt. Thousands lost jobs, budgets were slashed, and projects without guaranteed hits were shelved. Bands were forced to downsize, and lead singers were pushed into solo careers, leaving bands and groups to flounder. Crossover success, once a long-term strategized goal, was now an upfront necessity.[19] *The Death of Rhythm & Blues* cites a 1976 interview with CBS Black music head LeBaron Taylor inadvertently laying out the "crossover formula": taking a single, goosing sales to gold status (500,000) through urban formats, then super-serving it to "mainstream" radio formats.[20]

This was no mean feat: a *Billboard* analyst calculated only twenty-three soul/R&B tracks managed to land on the annual *Billboard* Hot 100 List, and the average #1 soul hit only reached as high as #22 on the pop charts.[21] Retreating from the innovative sounds that defined the 1970s for Black pop, performers were forced into diluting creativity, recycling hits, and jumping on bandwagons. George points out, crossover moves only served short term—for veteran Black acts, it actually accelerated the end of their viability in the market: "A black [artist] who crossed over could sell a humongous number of records. And the fact that so few succeeded didn't stifle the dream. For many black entertainers, chasing that dream was a fixation, and one that could destroy a career."[22]

For example, Earth, Wind & Fire, once an apex Pan-Africanist polyglot ensemble steeped in spiritual messaging and jazz foundation, transformed into culturally neutered disco-soul superheroes. Kool & The Gang traded rough Jersey City jazz-funk for polished discotheque sheen. The Commodores' homespun Tuskegee funk switched up to saccharine pop balladry in service to their one-time front man. Even pinnacle genius Stevie Wonder reined in his once-vanguard experimentation. The dice roll was: (a) if hardcore fans would follow, (b) if new Black fans would buy in, and (c) if White fans would even care.[23]

Contrary to rock hubris, disco didn't "die." Disco resurfaces cyclically and is resurgent in the 2020s, but as the 1970s waned, it went into the background. This made the Isleys' next move curious—they not only did a deep dive into disco, they literally doubled down. In August 1979, they released *Winner Takes All*, a double-album set, and put out three singles: "I Wanna Be with You" (#1 R&B), "Winner Takes All," and "It's a Disco Night (Rock Don't Stop)" (#27 R&B, #90 pop). There were no standout ballads, though

"How Lucky Am I" (Rudolph's piece that was made over into "For the Love of You") was finally placed. Side two, featuring "Life in the City," "It's A Disco Night (Rock Don't Stop)," and "(Can't You See) What You Do to Me?," was like an extended disco cut running the whole side of the disc. There were no message songs, save for the last two tracks, general exhortations of positivity: "Go for What You Know," and "Mind over Matter." *Winner* did well for a double set, peaking at #3 *Billboard* Soul and #14 *Billboard* Pop. But the album only went gold. It shipped platinum years later, but, for now, the Isleys' platinum streak suffered its first hiccup.

As the decade ended, The Isley Brothers closed the book on what was the most lucrative stretch of albums of their career with another million seller, *Go All the Way*, again recorded at Bearsville and released in April 1980. It was a return to basics, just six extended-play tracks—five dance cuts and one ballad. "Don't Say Goodnight (It's Time For Love)" became a staple in Quiet Storm, *Billboard* R&B #1 and #39 Pop, peaking at #8 on the *Billboard* Top 200. It was the only official release, although rogue urban jocks added, "Say You Will," a soaring guitar-laced funk track, and, "Here We Go Again," a mid-tempo love romp that hit #11 *Billboard* R&B. *Go All the Way* finished at #4 on *Billboard* R&B albums, and #89 on US *Billboard* Top 200.

The year, the decade, and an entire cultural era slammed shut in one fell swoop on a grim and solemn note: a little before 11:00 PM, October 8, 1980, former Beatle John Winston Lennon and his wife Yoko Ono, returning from a recording session at the Record Plant, were accosted in front of their home at the Dakota on Manhattan's Upper West

Side. Mark David Chapman, who hours earlier got Lennon to autograph his copy of the new album *Double Fantasy*, returned later that night and shot the musician four times. Lennon was rushed by police cruiser to nearby Roosevelt Hospital, where he was pronounced dead nearly a half hour later.

The Beatles maintained throughout their paradigm-shifting careers that they were foundationally influenced by the Isleys and that "Twist and Shout" was the catalyst that fostered their legend, one of the breakout singles on their debut EMI EP, *Please Please Me*, and a signature for their watershed Ed Sullivan appearance and Shea Stadium concerts. In the Bert Berns documentary, Paul McCartney says, "I told Ernie, 'If it were not for The Isley Brothers, The Beatles would still be in Liverpool.'"[24]

Lennon once declared,

> Chuck Berry is the greatest influence on Earth. So is Bo Diddley and so is Little Richard. There is not one White group on Earth that hasn't got their music in them, and that's all I ever listened to. The only White [*sic*] I ever listened to was [Elvis] Presley on his early records, and he was doing Black music. Presley was in Memphis—obviously, he was listening to Black music. I don't blame him for wanting to be that music—I wanted to be that.[25]

Lennon's murder symbolized many things, mostly the clarion call of whatever optimism and altruistic spirit that still lingered from the 1960s. Twenty years of malaise, cynicism, and avarice rotted it like a cancer—the unthinkable killing of a Beatle was like the attending surgeon calling the time of death. As it related to the Isleys, his passing cut another cord of their thread through rock and roll history. The absence of some modicum of recognition—never mind reciprocity—from American rock fans who'd long supplanted the originals with the copies in their minds, accentuated the fallacy of the crossover dream. It merely reaffirmed a mantra Ronald often invoked in discussing the Isleys' predicament: "Black music has always been confined in some corner."[26]

6
Footsteps in the Dark
The End of the 3+3 Era

The 1980s landscape found Black Americans facing a collective crisis of identity, direction, and burnout from perpetual socioeconomic struggle dating back to the discontent of the Nixon years, through stillborn Carter neoliberalism and economic debility, now intensified by the open hostility of Reaganomics and top-heavy "trickle down" policies. The baton of Black empowerment was left waiting for the next generation of energized and inspiring leaders to pick it up.

Black music always transitioned through generational divides, but with new genre forms emerging in the 1980s, the divide was more like an abyss. Older school, mainstream urban, and crossover offerings were seen by next-gen as dated and disconnected from issues and burgeoning trends within the community. The new underground music embraced by Black and LatinX teens and young adults—mostly hip-hop, but also reggae, punk, electro-funk, freestyle—reflected greater social attenuation, but mainstreamers saw it as too radical, offbeat, primitive, out-of-sync with haute couture, "lacking quality," and defiant of precedent.

Record companies, of course, profited selling *all* music to *all* sides: the conformists, the dissidents, and the disengaged. Changing times and attitudes goosed what would soon be the largest sales rush the industry ever experienced.[1] The biggest industry label, CBS Records (the Isleys' T-Neck parent), was poised for a historic windfall—whether The Isley Brothers would be part of it was another matter, as they (and other veteran Black artists) would struggle to find footing in a new environment.

The Isleys' new challenges were actually set in motion just after they signed. After Clive Davis was terminated in 1973, the future of CBS Records would be placed in the hands of a figure from his past: Walter Yetnikoff, Brooklyn-born son of Russian Jewish immigrants with a life path nearly identical to his benefactor. Graduate magna cum laude at Brooklyn College, followed by a degree at Columbia Law. After a two-year stint in the Army, he returned to the States and went to work at Rosenman, Colin, Kaye, Petschek, and Freund—the same firm Davis started at before joining CBS. In 1962, after Davis was made general counsel, Yetnikoff was hired as a staff attorney at his recommendation. When Davis was promoted, Yetnikoff took his general counsel position. After forging a joint venture with Sony, he became executive vice president of CBS Records International in 1969, then president of CBS Records International in 1971.[2]

Yetnikoff was there the day William S. Paley, CBS chairman, Arthur Taylor, CBS president, and the entire executive board were called to Taylor's 35th floor office at

"Black Rock," the ominous black marble tower in Rockefeller Center, and Taylor announced Davis' dismissal. Taylor was in a precarious spot: he and Davis clashed, but Davis had grown the records division to a third of the company's revenue. Not wanting to jeopardize profits, he needed a true records man to run the show. In May 1975, Taylor appointed Yetnikoff president of CBS Records.[3]

Yetnikoff was one of "The Suits," execs, like Davis, with no music background (typically, from law, management, business, finance, sales, marketing, and promotions), yet were running major music firms: Irving Azoff, David Geffen, Mo Ostin, Kenneth Glancy, and others. Yetnikoff, self-diagnosed as "tone deaf"—"I mean, I can't sing. My ear is okay, but somewhere between the ear and throat, there is something missing"[4]—had to lean into being a "character" to endear himself to his premiere talent. Once buttoned-down and reserved, he reinvented himself as "The Wild Man of Black Rock," a ferocious, fast-talking hustler, bare-knuckle brawler, and boardroom horror who'd terrorize any of the "suits" perceived as needlessly obtrusive. He presented as the ultimate peer and partner to his charges. This persona not only allowed him to manage roster expectations to the company's advantage but also put him at odds with its interests. Further, it drew him into a slipstream of destructive behaviors for both himself and CBS—booze, drugs, infidelity, partying, excessive spending, corporate alienation, and entanglement with payola schemes and purported mob figures (he was especially close to Morris Levy).[5] Yetnikoff's dealings were trained to give *him* the most leverage, by any means necessary. "Nobody," he boasted, "out-*geschrei* me."[6]

This shtick made Yetnikoff one of the most powerful (and perhaps feared) men in the business.

Yetnikoff's focus was CBS' top acts: Michael Jackson, Billy Joel, Earth, Wind & Fire, Bruce Springsteen, Barbra Streisand, The Rolling Stones, Paul McCartney, James Taylor, and so on, several of whom had multiple albums shipping eight figures. The vast majority of CBS Records' other acts, particularly the imprints, were handled by Epic execs Ron Alexenburg, senior vice president and general manager, and Steve Popovich, vice president of A&R. Both worked promotions until elevated to their respective posts in 1972. As most of CBS' Black performers were signed to or through Epic, Alexenberg, and Popovich were the principal handlers of urban talent.

There appears to be no record of the type of rapport Yetnikoff had, if any, with the Isleys. They aren't mentioned in any Yetnikoff interviews, nor is he mentioned in any of theirs. From all appearances, Yetnikoff, like all top music execs, concentrated on priorities of his choosing and delegated other matters to the rest of his team, as was his prerogative. Typically, if a matter arose involving an artist he had no direct relationship with, he left it to lower-tier administrators or issued an edict through an intermediary (one anecdote in his autobiography has him—perhaps jokingly—directing Tommy Motolla, his right hand, to have Living Colour fire their lawyer, Allen Grubman, in a beef over Michael Jackson's pending contract).[7] As to the Isleys' regard for CBS, Ernie said in a 1977 interview,

> Our relationship with [Columbia] is great. Before we came over, the most we'd sold on any album was 220,000.

We've done over a million copies on each of our Columbia albums. People said, "It's a big company, you'll get lost in the shuffle." But whatever else you can say about Columbia, there's one thing they know how to do, and that's sell records.[8]

The Isleys not making a huger impression higher up is curious. Yetnikoff was effusive about his affinity for Philly International (largely due to the hedonist lifestyle disco invoked): "Gamble and Huff were the creators of an edgy urban sensibility that blossomed into disco. As Motown led the sixties, Philly International was defining the seventies. And by mid-decade, that definition had everything to do with dancing and screwing."[9] But while Philly sold gangbusters on their top acts—The O'Jays, Harold Melvin & The Blue Notes, Teddy Pendergrass—the Isleys sold better than any artist there. Yetnikoff presided over the bulk of the group's platinum streak: the only Black artist at CBS (*not* named Michael Jackson) whom the Isleys trailed in sales was Earth, Wind & Fire. It's difficult to fathom that escaping his notice, especially after they'd been so public about their clashes with the AOR cognoscenti.

Nevertheless, the Isleys now sought the path of least resistance, leaning into mainstream R&B. In March 1981, the group put out *Grand Slam* without much fanfare—the promotional blitz usually accompanying Isley releases is absent. It was atypical of an Isleys' launch—the album cover didn't even use original photos, just repurposed pictures from *Showdown*. Critical reaction was lukewarm, mostly from urban publications (reviews of its reissue have been more positive). The recurring theme was the music was formulaic and uninspired. It's one thing for such critique to come from outsiders as in years past and quite another to get them from sympathetic scribes. The first side was ballads, except for the mid-tempo single, "Hurry Up and Wait," the album's biggest hit (#17 *Billboard R&B*, #58 *Billboard* Pop); and the second side was dance tracks. Two other singles were released, "Who Said" (#20 *Billboard* R&B) and "I Once Had Your Love (And I Can't Let Go)" (#57 *Billboard* R&B), and the album shipped gold, but it was still a setback after *Go All The Way* went platinum.

With little on record from the Isleys about *Grand Slam*, it's a knotty matter to discern the family mood during this period. Based on a few print interviews and random reports, almost all after the fact (there wasn't much press for *Grand Slam*), allusions were all was not ideal at the homestead. News items citing issues over creative direction, album credit, publishing, money, taxes, and finances surfaced here and there, with inconsistent details emerging years later about a rift between the older and younger siblings.

Still, the family put its best face forward. In December, the Isleys released *Inside You*, their twentieth studio album, again keeping pace with R&B trends. The group appeared dressed in ornate cowboy outfits. In a significant departure, the personnel expanded beyond the six-man format, employing strings, horns, and Everett Collins (drums) and Kevin Jones (congas) from the road band. They even cut a song from an outside writer, David Townsend, who contributed "First Love." Two singles were released: the title track (#10 *Billboard* R&B) and "Welcome into My Heart" (#45 *Billboard* R&B).

The album finished #8 on *Billboard* Top Soul albums and #45 on *Billboard* Pop albums. It didn't sell—their first album since they signed with CBS that didn't at least ship gold.

Entering 1982, several transformative events reshaped the industry (and created more challenges for the band). First was the introduction of compact disc (CD) technology, music digitally mastered to a disc a quarter-size of an album, yet holding twice the data. CDs reshaped how music was recorded, promoted, consumed, and experienced. Early price points for CDs and players were steep—the first players fetched up to $900, and CDs were $20 apiece.[10] Eventually prices came down enough for mass consumption, but CDs only dropped to $11 for re-releases and $16 for new releases—the average cost of a double album. The Recording Industry Association of America reasoned CDs should be priced as such—and even higher—regardless of whether its contents *totaled* a double album. In fact, vinyl prices were *raised* to match CDs—this, along with complaints from big box stores, brought huge fines against the majors from the Federal Trade Commission for price fixing.[11] Still, lower-income groups (Black, LatinX, etc.) were behind the curve adapting to CD tech and urban albums suffered a lag before matching other genres. Top sellers took precedence and it took time for many artists, especially Black artists, to rebound—many did not.

Another gamechanger was the launch of Music Television (MTV) on August 1, 1981. Formed by Warner-American Express Satellite Entertainment Company, MTV streamed music videos twenty-four hours a day with breaks for news, interviews, specials, events, and entertainment segments. It was developed by Robert W. Pittman, who became chairman and CEO of MTV Networks. Music videos were nothing new—they were used to promote station adds, sales pitches, conventions, and variety show segments. MTV standardized videos as both entertainment and art form. VH1 (Video Hits One) was added in 1985 as an adjunct adult contemporary channel to MTV. BET (Black Entertainment Television) started in 1980 but didn't begin airing videos until 1983.

MTV ran with an album-oriented rock format with pop acts mixed in (Madonna, Cyndi Lauper, Hall & Oates, Spandau Ballet), but the station wouldn't play popular Black artists. Pittman argued MTV was a rock-based station and they played Black rock artists—citing Jimi Hendrix, Joan Armatrading, and Gary US Bonds—but they were rarely in rotation, less so once the network assembled a more contemporized library.[12] Black artists had to rely on network TV, cable-access, and UHF to get their videos aired.

Motown funk rock artist Rick James, with one of the biggest albums of 1981—four times platinum *Street Songs*—set off a firestorm, publicly accusing MTV of racism.[13] Separately, David Bowie (who regularly collaborated with Black artists like Nile Rodgers and Luther Vandross) also called out MTV for not playing Black acts. In an infamous interview with stammering VJ Mark Goodman, Bowie blasted the network for its lack of diversity. Weakly defending MTV's stance, Goodman said, "We grew up in an era where The Isley Brothers meant something to me. But what does it mean to a 17-year-old?" Bowie replied, "I'll tell you what The Isley Brothers and Marvin Gaye mean to a *Black* 17-year-old, and surely he's part of America."[14] Only after Yetnikoff took MTV to task over Michael Jackson's videos did the network give in.

"I argued they were racist assholes, and I'd trumpet it to the world if they didn't relent. I've never been more forceful or obnoxious. I've also never been as effective, threatening to pull *all* our videos. With added pressure from Quincy Jones, they caved in."[15]

The Isleys didn't put out videos for a couple of years, so their onset didn't impact them. It did have consequences on label resources: videos were costly—in 1981, the average budget was $15,000, but by 1984, it ballooned to $40,000–$50,000.[16] Videos added nearly a quarter million dollars in marketing costs per artist (in many cases, more than the actual *production* budget), which meant even more pressure to sell records.

But the biggest shift was the onslaught of the album blockbuster, massive selling releases that absorbed much of the bandwidth of the media and record-buying public, and, consequently, demanded the lion's share of a label's time and resources. These albums were milked for as many singles as possible to keep the artist constantly in the public consciousness and maximize sales.[17] The year 1982 saw two such albums released within a month of each other: *1999* by Prince, October 27, and *Thriller* by Michael Jackson, November 29. And while *Thriller* would go on to be the largest-selling album in recording history (over 70 million units sold), at the time singles from both albums took turns holding pole position at the top of the charts. (Since *Thriller* ran over a four-year cycle, Prince actually released another blockbuster in September 1984, *Purple Rain*, and its attendant film, which extended the chart rivalry between the two stars.)

Soon the market was flush with blockbusters drowning out all else happening in music: *Toto IV* (Toto), *Tug of War* (Paul McCartney), *Hello, I Must Be Going* (Phil Collins), *Synchronicity* (The Police), *Pyromania* (Def Leppard), *Eliminator* (ZZ Top), *Colour by Numbers* (Culture Club), *Speaking in Tongues* (The Talking Heads), *Frontiers* (Journey), *Madonna* (Madonna), *Can't Slow Down* (Lionel Richie), and *Rio* (Duran Duran), with Jackson and Prince leading the way.

This made tough sledding for low-to-moderate selling acts. Such was definitely the case for the Isleys as, in August 1982, they put out *The Real Deal*, an effort to latch on to heavy electro-funk sounds prominent in Black pop. It continued the expanded arrangements: strings, Everett Collins and Kevin Jones on drums and percussion, and O'Kelly and Chris sharing co-leads with Ronald. Three singles were released, only charting on *Billboard* R&B: "The Real Deal" (#14), "It's Alright with Me" (#59), and "All in My Lover's Eyes" (#67). The album topped at #9 *Billboard* Top Soul and #87 *Billboard* Pop, but, again, failed to ship gold. Strangely, the Isleys signed their first outside act to T-Neck, soul music favorites Bloodstone of "Natural High" fame, with an album and single titled, "We Go a Long Way Back." The track had some success but didn't chart, and the follow-up album, *Party* in 1984, got no traction at all.

The Isleys' slump needs to be framed in a broader context: Black music was either crossing over, going to smoothed-out funk or electronic. New jacks replaced veterans not on trend. And hip-hop was on the rise. Many acts of the Isleys' generation were enduring similar slumps: Earth, Wind & Fire, Parliament-Funkadelic, Gladys Knight & The Pips,

Curtis Mayfield, Al Green, The Temptations, Sly Stone, and more.

But most importantly, the independent labels flooding the scene when the Isleys first broke—the vital gateway to Black music penetrating the American marketplace—had been bought out by majors or folded altogether. Atlantic had long been sold to Warners in 1967; Stax shuttered in 1975 after an extended legal battle with CBS; Philadelphia International imploded in 1984; Solar (formerly Soul Train) Records sold their interests and artists to Elektra and MCA; and, finally, the benchmark of Black pop, Motown, could no longer sustain escalating costs, signing a distribution deal with MCA in 1982, then selling outright to MCA and Boston Ventures Inc. in 1988. For many, this was the outcome portended in CBS' 1972 Harvard Report: the corporate takeover of the production, distribution, and promotion of Black popular music.[18] It was just the tip of the iceberg: giant corporations kept buying firms to where now only three majors control 85 percent of the industry: Universal Music Group, Sony Music Entertainment, and Warner Music Group, each representing a smaller component of a multimedia mega-conglomerate portfolio with much more vast holdings.[19]

The Isleys, already a tiny cog in a colossal machine, were now diminished even further, no matter how many records they sold. And, at this juncture, they weren't selling many at all. They went back to basics for their next album, *Between the Sheets*, stripping back down to the 3+3 format with no outside input. The sourcing of material was a point of contention, based on later interviews with Ernie, Chris, and Marvin: they'd been mulling a side project featuring the three of them since *Go All the Way*, but the songs ended up on Isley albums. There were disagreements about the younger members to taking leads, a nonstarter for the older brothers. As usual, everything was talked through and the group got to work. "We do have fights," said Ernie. "Because they're my brothers, I can tell them what I think. So, we disagree only to agree. I may give in on something I really don't like, but if so, it's for everybody's sake."[20]

Between the Sheets was released on April 24, 1983, and the title track was their biggest hit in years. The single reached *Billboard* R&B #3—informally an "answer" record to Marvin Gaye's recent smash, "Sexual Healing" (Gaye, sadly, died earlier that same month). The second release, "Choosey Lover," also did well, reaching *Billboard* R&B #6. Oddly, the Isleys made their first video on a cut that was never released, "Ballad for the Fallen Soldier," revisiting the group's rock roots and featuring Ernie's guitar wizardry. The album finished the year at #1 *Billboard* Top Soul and #19 *Billboard* Pop. Most importantly, it shipped a million copies—the group had their mojo back, at least for now.

In the bigger picture at CBS Records, there was only one thing happening in 1983: the juggernaut of Michael Jackson's second Epic release, *Thriller*. The album dominated every arena of popular culture for four straight years. It was in the Top Ten of seventeen international charts, #1 on eleven of them. Seven of the album's nine tracks were released as singles, all of which reached the *Billboard* Top Ten, setting the record for the most Top Ten releases from a single album. It won eight Grammys, including Album of the Year and Record of the Year. Jackson also submitted the boldest videos the new medium had ever seen (giving MTV—which ironically blocked his videos at first—legitimacy it would never have had otherwise). *Thriller* changed all conventional thinking about music, video, film, design, and popular culture.

What it changed most is the return-on-investment labels now demanded of artists. Sales from albums like *Thriller* were now seen as standard, not the once-in-a-lifetime exception they actually were. Artist development and grace periods for acts to settle into the marketplace were over and done: the attitude was "hits now or who's next." Underperforming artists were dropped outright or trapped in label purgatory, their work locked in company vaults and non-compete clauses preventing them from changing labels without hefty buyouts.[21]

If the Isleys' troubles were limited to such outside-world matters, they may have been able to weather them out. But they weren't—the problems the group needed to address now were internal. The personal finances of O'Kelly, Rudolph, and Ronald appeared to be one significant factor: according to a *Jet* magazine item dated September 13, 1979, reports of $663,000 in unpaid taxes, IRS liens, and seized properties had surfaced (a group spokesperson stated the Isleys were "aware and addressing the matter").[22] A *Forbes* report noted that the older brothers, through Ronald, filed for bankruptcy in 1984 (Ronald did so again in 1997).[23]

Creative differences also arose regarding the group's direction, publishing divisions, and proper crediting. While all agree that everything was discussed openly and honestly, the older brothers resisted many of the new ideas the younger guys were bringing to the table. "When you do things just because that's the way you always do things, and not for musical reasons, then it stops being about the music," said Chris. "And when it stops being about the music, it's time to quit."[24]

The older brothers had a different take. Ronald said CBS reportedly wanted two different Isley projects: one with the full group and one with the younger brothers. "It was the wrong time for two Isley albums," Ronald said. "It seemed like too much product at one time. We *really* wanted the younger members to record a separate album. But we didn't want them to do it then."[25]

This time, with neither side budging on their positions, neither able to continue the status quo nor find common ground, it was clear the 3+3 iteration of The Isley Brothers had run its course. So, the sad decision was made: The Isley Brothers were splitting, with the O.G.'s starting over and the Young Guns launching something fresh. "We were very straightforward about it," said Chris. "There weren't any hard feelings."[26] Ronald reflected, "They probably couldn't really do what they wanted when they were with us—the group wasn't structured for that. I was probably guilty of being too bossy to them. Eventually they were going to go off and do what they wanted. But when they left to form their own group, it was all very friendly."[27]

The year 1984 was the Isleys' twenty-fifth anniversary in the music business. It should have been a celebratory year— it wasn't. *Between the Sheets* should have been a triumphant comeback after three years of struggling—it wasn't. Their recent success should have been a catalyst to compete with all the blockbuster records on the scene (*Thriller* and *In Between the Sheets* were ranked #1 and #2 respectively in *Jet*'s Top 20 Albums)—it wasn't. And unbeknown to all at the time, this last platinum album would also be their final album ever with all six members. It was like the song off the *3+3* album that made everything possible ten years prior: you walk your way; I'll walk mine.

7
You Still Feel the Need

Of course, clearly, the breakup wasn't the end of The Isley Brothers' story. It merely marks the end of where the Isleys actively centered themselves as a rock and roll group—around *Go for Your Guns*, whereas thereafter, the group aggressively pursues Black pop as defined by the marketplace—thus, closing the area of concentration for this writing. Astonishingly, the official "3+3" era that made The Isley Legend—not counting 1969 through 1972, when Ernie, Chris, and Marvin were being groomed—only comprised *a single decade* of a seven-decade career of chart hits.

The path from the split to their latter-day renaissance was not without struggle: for a time, the family's post-*In Between the Sheets* offerings—as the original lineup, Isley-Jasper-Isley, and solo efforts (Ron, Ernie, and Chris)—yielded a few hits, but largely modest results, and the next few years were mired in false starts, missteps, and tragedy. Most notable were the losses of the oldest and youngest Isley Brothers—O'Kelly Jr., who suffered from a heart attack in March of 1986, and Marvin, who passed away from complications related to chronic diabetes in June of 2010. Rudolph left the group in 1987 to pursue the ministry in Chicago. After suffering a health scare from a mild stroke in 2004, Ronald was convicted on tax evasion charges in 2006 and served three years, splitting his sentence between Terre Haute, IN, and St. Louis, MO, where he and Ernie presently reside with their families. Chris Jasper runs his record label/production company, Gold City Records, out of Westchester County, NY. Sadly, Rudolph died of a heart attack in October 2023. But during this period, the Isleys also produced another wave of gold or platinum hits. Presently, they enjoy extended life as Black pop royalty and elder statesmen, passionately embraced by Generation Hip Hop/R&B, and authors of another string of million sellers, through new music, cameos, covers, or sampling.

Understanding that time-traveling back fifty-plus years for corrective discourse on a canon that never had proper vetting in its prime—in hopes of creating consensus in an even more divisive present—is the very definition of futility. But unlike The Beatles, The Stones, Zeppelin, or the vast majority of White rock icons, whose canons are encapsulated in a fixed time frame and sustained through ceaseless resurrection loops, the Isleys are still making relevant *current* music. And their catalog finds new converts each year via online. This *demands* a reassessment of the group's classic rock material (as well as *other* Black artists who've been excluded). This correction is mandatory for any valid discourse on rock music. As Eric Weisbard surmises, "Chronicling the Isley Brothers from the 1950s to the 2000s positions rock and roll, rhythm and blues (R&B) and Top 40 as three sometimes joined, sometimes clashing long histories.[1]"

The music industry's profit-driven myopia, trained on codified, regimented modes for Black expression, is *squarely and inherently* responsible for the fractured and reductive grasp of Black culture and the anemic choices Black artists are forced to make to sustain careers. These abstract standards— *STILL NOT COGENTLY DEFINED by any measure other than race, gender, or culture stereotypes*—have corrupted any rational attempt at intersectional exchange for non-White, non-male, non-binary, or non-Judeo-Christian creatives (i.e., farces like "Jimi Hendrix, Stevie Wonder aren't 'Black'"). As Jack Hamilton states in *Just around Midnight: Rock and Roll and the Racial Imagination*, "No Black-derived musical form in American history has more assiduously moved to erase and blockade Black participation than rock music. When rock ideology purged itself of (visible) Blackness, it was foreclosing not simply African American performers but an entire young tradition of interracial fluidity."[2]

The Talk: It's Time for Truth-Telling about Race and Rock and Roll

It is universally documented that rock music was hewn predominantly from Black root forms and musical systems bedrock to Americana, gospel, blues, and jazz, and informed by the Black experience from slavery to the present day.[3] Yet even its highest-profile Black figures are reduced to footnotes or redacted entirely, never commanding the marketplace. Only in recent years have Black artists achieved comparable acclaim and remuneration as White artists, due mainly to the rise of hip-hop/R&B as the highest-selling genre globally since 2017, according to *Billboard*.[4] Historian and ethnomusicologist Reebee Garofalo notes, "The specific practices and mechanisms that tend to institutionalize [Black music's] exclusion and dilution change over time and, for the most part, remain unchallenged even to this day."[5]

Who "Owns" Rock Culture?

Nearly all cultural surveys of rock music, while guardedly conceding its Black pioneers and social points of origin, place dogged emphasis on "cultural fluidity" and miscegenation, diminishing the essentiality and insolubility of Black culture within genres. Of note, Fredric Dannen's seminal *Hit Men*, states:

> Pop in the industry is a euphemism for White; R&B means Black. A rock record by a Black act is automatically R&B—regardless of its *sound*—unless White radio plays it and White people buy it, at which point it is said to 'cross over' to the pop charts. Since White record buyers outnumber Blacks by a large margin, a crossover hit means a bigger payoff.[6]

This premise, like most analyses of rock's permeation in the American consciousness (and Black pop's inverse constraints), depicts these trends as a clinical matter: typical benign aesthetic shifts resisted initially by obsoleting modes and quorums that invariably acquiesce to newer ones. But the simplistic "majority-minority" pretext that professionals, scholars, critics, historians, and analysts rely on presumes a neutrality that *never* existed. The sociological condition of

Black and White power dynamics in America supersedes mere numbers—Black culture's penetration and advancement into larger spheres has always been a *diametrically and ferociously opposed* function, with White dominance the presumed default setting.

From slavery, through minstrelsy and industrialization, control positions were categorically those of government, business, and institutional guardians. Society's conjecture (and manifest political reality) was Black people had neither the acumen *nor the right* to warrant any consideration beyond goods and labor—Black opinion, as such, was utterly inconsequential.[7] Sociologist Charles Crowe notes: "Among the key conceptions of black culture for [leading white scholars], Southerners and white Americans generally were ideas about inherently 'backward levels of development,' innate 'temperament,' biological 'nature'—and the benefits of white power to an 'inferior' people with 'uncivilized' origins."[8]

The key tenet to music's profitability is affirmation of societal "norms" (White authority, Black sublimation), hence the unchallenged metamorphoses of "race music" to "jump blues," to "rhythm and blues," to "rock and roll," to White immersion and Black expulsion, to separate designations of rock and rhythm and blues, and all subsequent subgenres of each. In her essay "Music, Power, and Practice," ethnomusicologist and educator Maureen Mahon writes: "These seemingly neutral categories are underwritten by socially constructed ideas about which types of people should participate in which musical forms. Furthermore, these genre classifications are informed by the ways we think about identity beyond the realm of music, and they in turn affect the ways we think about identity beyond that realm."[9]

Until the expansion of Black cultural critique in the 1950s, 1960s, and 1970s, genre designation was the exclusive purview of venture capitalists and White cultural stewards. Black people didn't invent tropes like "jazz," "rhythm and blues" or "rock and roll" (all euphemisms for sex). Artists shrugged off or chafed at such terms, unless there was some material benefit attached. Chuck Berry mused, "It used to be called boogie woogie, it used to be called the blues, used to be called rhythm and blues. It's rock now."[10] Further, the notion of "cultural fluidity" becomes specious given the historic freedom of White artists to engage and succeed in popular "Black genres," and the vociferous restraint upon Black artists engaging in so-called "nontraditional genres," criterion set along social delineations rather than stylistic.[11]

Who Paid the Cost to Be the Boss?

But of graver significance, the path to rock's assimilation was far more mordant than a mere aesthetic shift. The genre itself was *criminalized explicitly* for its roots in Black community and the mass hysteria of its purported influence on White children—its transition into the mainstream was fraught with trauma, propaganda, violence, and active retribution against Black lives. These were *institutional* directives—in Southern *and* Northern states—by White legislators, law enforcement, business leaders, educators, churches, and "concerned citizens groups." The gamut ran from Birmingham White Citizens Council head Asa "Ace" Carter, charging rock and roll—"the basic heavy-beat music of the Negroes"—appealed to "the base in man, brings out animalism and vulgarity," and represented a plot to "mongrelize America,"[12] to neoliberal Massachusetts congressman Tip O'Neill, arguing rock and roll was "a type of sensuous music unfit for impressionable minds."[13] (Carter and other White supremacists even conflated rock music with civil rights in an effort to discredit the movement.)

Bans were imposed, concerts and dances shut down, radio stations and record stores censored, picketed, and fined. Performers, DJs, and promoters were threatened, harassed, attacked, and arrested. Raids, riots, record and book burnings, curfews, sundowner laws, anti-dance ordinances, chaperone laws, jukebox laws, segregated events, campaigns, town hall meetings, PTA meetings, church meetings, local, state, and federal hearings, mainstream media (including *Billboard* and *Cashbox*), all conspired against rock and roll (and, to varying degrees, the Black people behind the music).[14] Yes, White practitioners did suffer consequences, but with nowhere near the severity and impunity of those against Black practitioners.

White performers also reaped exponentially greater benefits: rock's profiteers were marginally more beneficent than its detractors—innumerable millions were made exploiting legions of Black performers who never saw rewards equitable to the White performers who copied and supplanted them. Countless acts like Wynonie Harris, Ruth Brown, Muddy Waters, Lavern Baker, Frankie Lymon, et al. all died penniless. Sam Phillips, Elvis' discoverer, got his million-dollar "White man with the Black sound," but Arthur "Big Boy" Crudup and Willie Mae "Big Mama" Thorton, whose hits launched Elvis to fame, never had two nickels to rub together between them. This is the rawest nerve in any discourse that neuters the role race plays in rock: the worth of Black contributions, sacrifices, and lack of reparations has been irretrievably obfuscated.[15]

Work to Do

The rock music establishment—indeed the music business *as a whole*—is a century delinquent in providing full account to all the Black artists who, in creating these lucrative platforms, were summarily exploited and cast aside. In *not* doing this work and hiding behind rationales such as "market demand" and "demographics," the industry surrenders authority as cultural stewards, exposing its actual mercenary intent and function as cultural profiteers, demanding greater transparency and candor.

Every human's history is their absolute, divinely bestowed, irrevocable birthright. No person, no community, no government, no enterprise, no system has any right to mitigate that. Even late contrarian Lester Banks—renowned provocateur for publications like *Punk* and *Creem*—affirmed in his infamous Village Voice essay, "White Noise Supremacists," about racism in punk: "most of the greatest, deepest music America has produced has been, when not entirely black, the product of miscegenation. You can't appreciate rock 'n roll without appreciating where it comes from."[16]

Epilogue

After sixty-seven years, where the Isleys go from here has long stopped being in question. Here and now is the "phase" the Isleys are *always* at, and wherever they land next will likely be wherever Black popular music is at that time. And whether they ever record another note of rock music is beside the point. Because the Isleys are still relevant—their legacy, though not as pronounced as it should be, is very much assured. What is *not* as assured—and the whole impetus for this writing—is their true place in *history*. Not just R&B, soul, funk, or hip-hop history (or whatever Black history White folks will ignore because they don't feel it affects them).

Rock and roll history. Because the Isleys *are* rock and roll history—*living and breathing* rock and roll history. The rock music establishment tried its damnedest to deny them that. It's time for the rock music establishment to start paying back the Isleys—and a legion of other Black rock artists—what it owes them: respect. *Massive* respect. Retroactively. With interest. Forever. The clock starts right now. . . .

The Isley Brothers are, indisputably, America's longest-tenured, most venerable, active rock and roll group. Not R&B group. Not funk group. Not soul group. *Rock and roll* group. Y'all *really* need to start dealing with this . . . Everything ever signified about rock and roll has absolutely no validity or grounding until you do . . .

Addendum

Testimonials

VERNON REID, Living Colour, Black Rock Coalition cofounder
"It's always been a thing with me that Ernie Isley has never been on the cover of a significant guitar or music magazine of record. He's never gotten his due. And I have to ask, 'Why?' He is absolutely in the 'heir apparent' conversation with Hendrix—he was an eyewitness to Hendrix' becoming. He's got credentials, hit records. What more can you ask for? Ernie has been done a grave disservice."

JIMI HAZEL, 24-7 Spyz/Sepia XL
"Everybody is always trying to create types and zones to describe the way we do our music. The Isleys never gave themselves a type and neither did anybody else. It was just, 'The Isley Brothers.' They didn't *use* a type. They *were* a type. 'The Isley Brothers' said it all."

"CAPTAIN" KIRK DOUGLAS, The Roots/One Hundred Watt Heart

"The Isley Brothers symbolize crossroads of funk, soul, pop, rock 'n' roll and hip hop. The same group gave us 'Shout,' 'It's Your Thing,' 'Fight the Power,' and 'Who's That Lady?' Not to mention all those baby-making ballads that are part of the American fabric, both in their original form and by way of sampling in iconic rap classics. This band's breadth serves as a soundtrack to the Black experience in America."

RICKEY VINCENT, The Funk Professor (San Francisco State University), Host of "History of the Funk" (KPFA-FM, Pacifica Radio)

"Black radio revered these guys, so they were legends. I enjoyed their singles. Then 'Who's That Lady' happened. Everything I was programmed for had to be rebooted. These guys were doing rock for soul music in a way that had never been done. This said, 'You can dig it in the moment, but here's two colliding worlds we are making happen for you right now.' I said, 'Wait, I *love* this! But you're breaking all the rules!' This was a demarcation point where music could never be what it was on Black radio."

BOB DAVIS, founder of Soul-Patrol.com

"The Isley Brothers have always been the kind of multigenerational entity that spans musical styles and trends. In the Black community, it's possible for the entire family, from great-grandparents to toddlers, to get down to The Isley Brothers and have a different favorite song from a different era of the Isleys' career."

SANDRA ST. VICTOR, The Family Stand/Mack Diva
"'I try to play my music / They say the music's too loud.' The fact that I had to turn the volume knob down on the word 'bullshit' (within earshot of my Dad) on 'Fight The Power' made The Isley Brothers hit my edgy teenage sensibilities different. I was different. So were they. It was 1975. Teen angst, the juxtaposition of peace, love, and cuss words, of creamy falsetto against a screaming guitar equaled my heaven."

KEVIN GOINS, writer, researcher, radio programmer, historian, podcaster
"Here's the irony: the radio programmers and record promoters at that time were putting the Isleys in the R&B category because they were Black, end of story. Yet, you had these rock bands that were lifting Isley songs for their own singles: The Outsiders, Human Beinz, Joey Dee & The Starliters, The Yardbirds, all covering Isley original songs. Which showed that, 'Okay, you've pigeon-holed the Isleys to R&B, but you've got all these straight-up rock bands that are lifting their stuff.'"

LEAH KING, Independent multidiscipline artist, educator
"I downloaded 'Ohio/Machine Gun' from Napster when I was in college, and listened to it very regularly when I was living in racist Boston. It had the perfect balance of rhythm 'n' rock instrumentation, freestyled soulful vocals, and furious emotion that helped me manage my anger and turn it into productive rage, because, as Audre Lorde says, 'Anger is a grief of distortions between peers, and its object is change.'"

References

Essential Isley Brothers Albums

1. *The Isley Brothers 3+3* (1973)
2. *Go for Your Guns* (1977)
3. *Givin' It Back* (1971)
4. *Brother Brother Brother* (1972)
5. *The Heat Is On* (1975)
6. *Live It Up* (1974)
7. *Harvest for the World* (1976)
8. *The Isleys Live* (1973)
9. *It's Your Thing: The Story of the Isley Brothers* (1999)
10. *Wild in Woodstock: Live in Bearsville Sound Studio* (1980)

Essential Isley Brothers Singles

1. This Old Heart of Mine Is Weak for You
2. It's Your Thing
3. Twist and Shout
4. Shout
5. Who's That Lady? (Bert Berns' version)
6. Behind a Painted Smile
7. Take Me in Your Arms (Rock Me a Little While)
8. Testify (Pt. 1&2)

9. Hurry Up and Wait

10. Respectable

11. Right Now

12. Time After Time

13. The Cow Jumped over the Moon

14. I Wanna Know

15. Holding Back the Years

16. You've Got a Friend w/Aretha Franklin

17. If You Leave Me Now

18. Whispers (Getting Louder)

19. Feel Like the World

20. I Turned You On

The Isley Brothers websites: officialisleybrothers.com; ri-topten.com

Chris Jasper/Gold City Records website: goldcityrecords.com

A couple of very extensive write-ups have been extremely valuable in my research of the Isleys:

CD Booklet For "It's Your Thing: The Story of the Isley Brothers," Sony/Legacy, 1999.

"The Isley Brothers: We-e-e-e-e-ell!," Ben Simmons, *MOJO*, January 2000 (Rock's Back Pages).

"The Isley Brothers," Tony Cummings, *Black Music*, September 1973 (Rock's Back Pages).

"The Isley Brothers: The First Family of Soul," Steve Roeser, *Goldmine*, Volume 17, No. 24, Issue 296 (November 29, 1991).

Rock's Backpages is an archive of extensive articles, reviews, and interviews of noted figures in rock music, including several articles on The Isley Brothers: rocksbackpages.com

Notes

Introduction

1. Terkel, Studs. "An Interview with James Baldwin." *Conversations with James Baldwin*, edited by Fred L. Standley and Louis H. Platt (University Press of Mississippi, 1989), pp. 5–6.

2. Isley, Rudolph, Isley, O'Kelly, Isley, Ronald, Isley, Ernie, Isley, Marvin, and Jasper, Chris. "Fight the Power" (Bovina Music Publishing, 1975).

3. Strauss, Neil. MUSIC REVIEW: "Pop Veterans: Still Giving, Still Taking," *New York Times*, July 26, 1996, Section C, p. 16 (nytimes.com/1996/07/29/arts/music-review-pop-veterans-still-giving-still-taking.html).

4. Isley Brothers, bestsellingalbums.org.

5. McNeill, Darrell. Ernie Isley Interview Notes for BRE Magazine, 1999.

6. Hevesi, Dennis. "Marvin Isley, 56, Bassist in Isley Brothers," *New York Times*, June 8, 2010, Section B, p. 15 (nytimes.com/2010/06/08/arts/music/08isley.html).

7. Darling, Cary. "Why Aren't The Isley Brothers Worshipped as the Rock Gods They Are?" *The Houston Chronicle*, January 11,

2022 (preview.houstonchronicle.com/music/why-aren-t-the-isley-brothers-worshipped-as-the-16751754).

8. Porter, James. "Why Haven't The Isley Brothers Conquered the Rock Market?" *Chicago Reader*, July 16, 2019 (chicagoreader.com/music/why-havent-the-isley-brothers-conquered-the-rock-market).

9. Terich, Jeff. "A Beginner's Guide to the Funk-Soul of The Isley Brothers," *Treble Media,* February 11, 2022.

10. Darling. *The Houston Chronicle*, January 11, 2022.

11. *Billboard Top 100* (billboard.com).

12. Weisbard, Eric. *Top 40 Democracy: The Rival Mainstreams of American Music* (The University of Chicago Press, 2014), pp. 219–20.

13. McNeill, Darrell. Ernie Isley Interview Notes for BRE Magazine, 1999.

Chapter 1

1. Drozdz, Maya. "Village of Lincoln Heights," *Cincinnati Sites and Stories* (https://stories.cincinnatipreservation.org/items/show/111).

2. Semuels, Alana. "The Destruction of a Black Suburb," *The Atlantic*, July 13, 2015 (theatlantic.com/business/archive/2015/07/lincoln-heights-black-suburb).

3. Edmonds, Ben. "The Isley Brothers: We-e-e-e-e-e-ell!," *MOJO*, January 2000 (rocksbackpages.com/Library/Article/the-isley-brothers-we-e-e-e-e-e-elll).

4. CBS Sunday Morning, "'Amateur Night' at the Apollo, Now 80 Years Young," June 22, 2014 (cbsnews.com/news/amateur-night-at-the-apollo-now-80-years-young).

5. Edmonds. "The Isley Brothers," *MOJO*, January 2000.

6. Cummings, Tony. "The Isley Brothers," *Black Music*, 1973 (rocksbackpages.com/Library/Article/the-isley-brothers-3).

7. Cummings. "The Isley Brothers."

8. Tobler, John. *NME Rock 'N' Roll Years* (1st ed.) (London: Reed International Books Ltd., 1992), p. 211.

9. Hogan, Ed. "Hugo Peretti Biography," AllMusic.com.

10. Edmonds. "The Isley Brothers," *MOJO*, January 2000.

11. Hogan. "Hugo Peretti Biography."

12. Hogan. "Hugo Peretti Biography."

13. Edmonds. "The Isley Brothers," *MOJO*, January 2000.

14. Hogan. "Hugo Peretti Biography."

15. Bordowitz, Hank. "Ahmet Ertegun and the History of Atlantic Records," 1991 (teachrock.org/article/ahmet-ertegun-and-the-history-of-atlantic-records).

16. Bordowitz. "Ahmet Ertegun and the History of Atlantic Records."

17. Berns, Brett and Sarles, Bob. "Bang! The Burt Berns Story," 2016 (HCTN, Ravin' Films).

18. Berns and Sarles. "Bang! The Burt Berns Story."

19. Edmonds. "The Isley Brothers," *MOJO*, January 2000.

20. Berns and Sarles. "Bang! The Burt Berns Story."

21. Runtagh, Jordan. "Jimi Hendrix: 10 Great Pre-Fame Tracks," *Rolling Stone (rollingstone.com)*, November 17, 2017 (rollingstone.com/music/music-lists/jimi-hendrix-10-great-pre-fame-tracks).

22. Online interview, "Jimi Hendrix Black Legacy Retrospective," featuring Ernie Isley, Corey Washington,

Darrell M. McNeill, Bob Davis, Soul-Patrol.com, September 18, 2022.

23. Runtagh. *Rolling Stone.*

24. Jackson, Kourtnee. "The Isley Brothers Gave Jimi Hendrix One of His First Major Gigs," *Showbiz CheatSheet*, April 7, 2021 (cheatsheet.com/entertainment/the-isley-brothers-gave-jimi-hendrix-one-of-his-first-major-gigs).

25. Runtagh. *Rolling Stone.*

26. Barker, Andrew. "Holland-Dozier-Holland Receive a Star on the Hollywood Walk of Fame," *Variety*, February 13, 2015 (variety.com/2015/music/spotlight/holland-dozier-holland-receive-a-star-on-the-hollywood-walk-of-fame).

27. Gordy, Berry. *To Be Loved: The Music, The Magic, The Memories of Motown* (Headline Book Publishing, 1994), pp. 276–303.

28. Gordy. *To Be Loved.*

29. Gordy. *To Be Loved.*

Chapter 2

1. Ginsburg, Stewart. *It's Our Thing* liner notes, back cover (Reprinted from R 'n' B World, 1969).

2. Peck, Abe. "The Isley Brothers Are Ready for the Next Phase," *Rolling Stone*, Issue no. 271, August 10, 1978, pp. 8–16.

3. Ginsburg. *It's Our Thing* liner notes, back cover.

4. Pinnock, Tom. "The Isley Brothers—Inside the Group It Was like a Police State," *UNCUT*, March 31, 2017 (uncut.co.uk/features/isley-brothers-inside-group-like-police-state-99850).

5. Gonzales, Michael A. "Interview: Chris Jasper on Playing Synths for the Isleys," *Red Bull Music Academy Daily*, January 20, 2015 (redbull.com).

6. Hyde, Bob. "The Kama Sutra/Buddah Records Story," Both Sides Now Publications, 1993 (bsnpubs.com/buddah/buddahstory.html).

7. Edmonds, Ben. "The Isley Brothers: We-e-e-e-e-e-ell!," MOJO, January 2000 (rocksbackpages.com/Library/Article/the-isley-brothers-we-e-e-e-e-e-elll).

8. Isley v. Motown Record Corp., United States District Court for the Southern District of New York, 69 F.R.D. 12 (1975) (Quimbee.com).

9. Isley v. Motown Record Corp., United States District Court for the Southern District of New York, 69 F.R.D. 12 (1975) (Quimbee.com).

10. Online interview, "Jimi Hendrix Black Legacy Retrospective," featuring Ernie Isley, Corey Washington, Darrell M. McNeill, Bob Davis, Soul-Patrol.com, September 18, 2022.

11. Gibbs, Vernon. "3+3 = Super Success," *Essence*, May 1975 (rocksbackpages.com/Library/Article/the-isley-brothers-3--3--super-success).

12. Sampson, Kim. *Early 70s Radio: The American Format Revolution* (The Continuum International Publishing Corp., 2011), pp. 122–4.

13. Sampson. *Early 70s Radio*, pp. 122–4.

14. Gibbs. "3+3 = Super Success."

15. Amorsi, A. D. "In Conversation: It's Ernie Isley's Thing, He Does What He Wants to Do," *Flood Magazine*, October 8, 2015 (floodmagazine.com/24448/in-conversation-its-ernie-isleys-thing-he-does-what-he-wants-to-do).

16. Hyde. "The Kama Sutra/Buddah Records Story."

17. Hyde. "The Kama Sutra/Buddah Records Story."

18. Hyde. "The Kama Sutra/Buddah Records Story."

19. Hyde. "The Kama Sutra/Buddah Records Story."

Chapter 3

1. Tobler, John. *NME Rock 'N' Roll Years* (1st ed.) (London: Reed International Books Ltd., 1992), p. 48.

2. Schoemer, Karen. "Great Pretenders: My Strange Love Affair with '50s Pop Music," *Free Press*, New York, September 22, 2006 (archive.org/details/greatpretendersm00scho).

3. Garafalo, Reebee. "Crossing Over: From Black Rhythm & Blues to White Rock 'N' Roll," *Rhythm and Business: The Political Economy of Black Music* (Akashit Books, 2002), pp. 112–37.

4. Aswad, Jem. "Clive Davis Shares 'Clive-Isms' on Music, Artists, His History, and Keeping an Open Mind," *Variety*, April 6, 2022 (variety.com/2022/music/news/clive-davis-cliveisms-wisdom-music).

5. George, Nelson. *The Death of Rhythm and Blues* (Penguin Books, 1988), pp. 135–8.

6. Edmonds, Ben. "The Isley Brothers: We-e-e-e-e-ell!," MOJO, January 2000 (rocksbackpages.com/Library/Article/the-isley-brothers-we-e-e-e-e-elll).

7. Kubernik, Harvey. "The Heat's Still on the Isleys," *Melody Maker*, October 11, 1975 (rocksbackpages.com/Library/Article/isley-brothers-heats-still-on-isleys).

8. Kubernik. "The Heat's Still on the Isleys."

9. Valentine, Penny. "Stevie Wonder: Stevie's Moog Music," *Sounds*, Issue 22, January 1972 (rocksbackpages.com/Library/Article/stevie-wonder-stevies-moog-music).

10. Gonzales, Michael A. "Interview: Chris Jasper on Playing Synths for the Isleys," *Red Bull Music Academy Daily*, January 20, 2015 (daily.redbullmusicacademy.com/2015/01/chris-jasper-interview).

11. Amorsi, A. D. "In Conversation: It's Ernie Isley's Thing, He Does What He Wants to Do," *Flood Magazine*, October 8, 2015 (floodmagazine.com/24448/in-conversation-its-ernie-isleys-thing-he-does-what-he-wants-to-do).

12. Pinnock, Tom. "The Isley Brothers—Inside the Group It Was Like a Police State," *UNCUT*, March 31, 2017 (uncut.co.uk/features/isley-brothers-inside-group-like-police-state-99850).

13. Pinnock. "The Isley Brothers."

14. Pinnock. "The Isley Brothers."

15. Nicole, Shelley. Liner notes, *Harvest for the World* Reissued Vinyl, Big Break Records (Cherry Red Records, 2011). (All tracks licensed from Sony Music Entertainment UK Ltd.)

16. Edmonds. "The Isley Brothers."

17. Weisbard, Eric. *Top 40 Democracy: The Rival Mainstreams of American Music* (The University of Chicago Press, 2014), p. 57.

18. Pinnock. "The Isley Brothers."

19. Pinnock. "The Isley Brothers."

20. Pinnock. "The Isley Brothers."

21. Feretti, Fred. "C.B.S. Ousts an Executive and Sues Him for $94,000," *New York Times*, May 30, 1973 (New York Times Archives/nytimes.com).

22. Gonyea, Don. "Clive Davis: A Life with a Soundtrack," *The Record: Music News with NPR*, February 22, 2013 (npr.org/sections/therecord/2013/02/23/172719492/clive-davis-a-life-with-a-soundtrack).

23. Columbia Records Promotional Advertisement for *The Isley Brothers 3+3*, in *Billboard*, June 23, 1973.

24. Christgau, Robert. "Consumer Guide Reviews: The Isley Brothers" (robertchristgau.com/get_artist.php?name=The+Isley+Brothers).

25. Cummings, Tony. "The Isley Brothers," *Black Music*, December 1973 (Rock's Backpages).

26. Gibbs, Vernon. "3+3 = Super Success," *Essence*, May 1975 (Rock's Backpages).

Chapter 4

1. Sampson, Kim. *Early 70s Radio: The American Format Revolution* (The Continuum International Publishing Corp., 2011), pp. 120–4.

2. Sampson. *Early 70s Radio.*

3. Sampson. *Early 70s Radio.*

4. Sampson. *Early 70s Radio.*

5. Sampson. *Early 70s Radio.*

6. Nathan, David. "Go for Your Guns, Amigo. Them Thar Isleys Are Back in Town with a New Album," *Blues & Soul*, October 25, 1977 (rocksbackpages.com/Library/Article/go-for-your-guns-amigo-them-thar-isleys-are-back-in-town-with-a-new-album).

7. Rapp, Alison. "45 Years Ago: The Rolling Stones Embrace Disco on 'Miss You,'" Ultimate Classic Rock, May 10, 2023 (ultimateclassicrock.com/the-rolling-stones-miss-you).

8. Weisbard, Eric. *Top 40 Democracy: The Rival Mainstreams of American Music* (The University of Chicago Press, 2014), pp. 28–69.

9. Weisbard. *Top 40 Democracy.*

10. Weisbard. *Top 40 Democracy.*

11. Ofori, Kofi Asiedu. *FCC Report: "When Being Number 1 Is Not Enough,"* December 15, 1998.

12. Speed, Bill. Black Radio Column, *Radio & Records*, Issue # 283, May 25, 1979.

13. Roeser, Steve. "The Isley Brothers: The First Family of Soul," *Goldmine Magazine*, Issue #296, November 29, 1991.

14. Nathan. *Blues & Soul.*

15. Pinnock, Tom. "The Isley Brothers—Inside The Group It Was Like a Police State," *UNCUT,* March 31, 2017 (uncut.co.uk/features/isley-brothers-inside-group-like-police-state-99850)

16. Isley, Ernie, Isley, Marvin, Jasper, Chris, Isley, Rudolph, Isley, O'Kelly, and Isley, Ronald. "Fight the Power" (Bovina Music Publishing, 1975).

17. Harrell, Phil. "'Fight the Power': A Tale of 2 Anthems: With the Same Name," *Morning Edition* (NPR), December 7, 2018 (npr.org/programs/morning-edition/2018/12/07/674459902/morning-edition-for-december-7-2018).

18. Kubernik, Harvey. "The Heat's Still on the Isleys," *Melody Maker*, October 11, 1975 (rocksbackpages.com/Library/Article/isley-brothers-heats-still-on-isleys).

19. Edmonds, Ben. "The Isley Brothers: We-e-e-e-e-e-ell!," *MOJO*, January 2000 (rocksbackpages.com/Library/Article/the-isley-brothers-we-e-e-e-e-e-elll).

20. Kubernik. *Melody Maker*.

21. Edmonds. "The Isley Brothers," *MOJO*, January 2000.

22. Kubernik. *Melody Maker*.

23. Edmonds. "The Isley Brothers," *MOJO*, January 2000.

24. White, Cliff. "The Isley Brothers: *Go for Your Guns* (Epic)," *New Musical Express*, July 9, 1977 (rocksbackpages.com/Library/Article/the-isley-brothers-go-for-your-guns-epic).

25. Simpson, Dave. "How the Isley Brothers Made 'Harvest for the World,'" *The Guardian*, July 6, 2020 (theguardian.com/music/2020/jul/06/ernie-and-ron-isley-how-we-made-harvest-for-the-world-isley-brothers).

26. Pinnock. "The Isley Brothers."

27. Gonzales, Michael A. "Interview: Chris Jasper on Playing Synths for the Isleys," *Red Bull Music Academy Daily*, January 20, 2015 (daily.redbullmusicacademy.com/2015/01/chris-jasper-interview).

28. Isley, Rudolph, Isley, O'Kelly, Isley, Ronald, Isley, Ernie, Isley, Marvin, and Jasper, Chris. "Harvest For The World" (Bovina Music Publishing, 1976).

29. Sigerson, Davitt. "Ernie Isley: Pride of the Isleys," *Black Music*, September 1977 (rocksbackpages.com/Library/Article/ernie-isley-pride-of-the-isleys).

30. Gonzales. *Red Bull Music Academy Daily*.

31. Nathan. *Blues & Soul*.

32. Sigerson. *Black Music*.

33. Isley, Ernie, Isley, Marvin, Jasper, Chris, Isley, Rudolph, Isley, O'Kelly, Isley, and Ronald, Isley. "The Pride" (Bovina Music Publishing, 1977).

34. Isley, Ernie, Isley, Marvin, Jasper, Chris, Isley, Rudolph, Isley, O'Kelly, and Isley, Ronald. "Footsteps In The Dark" (Bovina Music Publishing, 1977).

35. Isley, Ernie, Isley, Marvin, Jasper, Chris, Isley, Rudolph, Isley, O'Kelly, and Isley, Ronald. "Voyage to Atlantis" (Bovina Music Publishing, 1977).

36. Isley, Ernie, Isley, Marvin, Jasper, Chris, Isley, Rudolph, Isley, O'Kelly, and Isley, Ronald. "Living In The Life" (Bovina Music Publishing, 1977).

37. White. *New Musical Express*.

38. Nathan. *Blues & Soul*.

Chapter 5

1. Peck, Abe. "The Isley Brothers Are Ready for the Next Phase," *Rolling Stone*, Issue no. 271, August 10, 1978, pp. 8–16 (Cues 1 through 3).

2. Peck. *Rolling Stone*.

3. Peck. *Rolling Stone*.

4. Garafalo, Reebee. "Crossing Over: From Black Rhythm & Blues to White Rock 'N' Roll," in *Rhythm and Business: The Political Economy of Black Music* (Akashit Books, 2002), pp. 112–37.

5. Weisbard, Eric. *Top 40 Democracy: The Rival Mainstreams of American Music* (The University of Chicago Press, 2014), pp. 28–69.

6. Weisbard. *Top 40 Democracy*.

7. Weisbard. *Top 40 Democracy*.

8. Weisbard. *Top 40 Democracy*.

9. Interview with Bill "Rosko" Mercer on WBAI-FM, *Creative Unity Collective Show*, WBAI 99.5-FM, New York, 1987 (WBAI Radio Archives: wbai.org/archive/).

10. Maultsby, Portia K. Ph.D. "Disco," *Timeline of African American Music*, Carnegie Hall cultural database, 2021 (timeline.carnegiehall.org/genres/disco).

11. Weisbard. *Top 40 Democracy*, pp. 28–69.

12. Petridis, Alexis. "Disco Demolition: The Night They Tried to Crush Black Music," *The Guardian*, July 19, 2019 (theguardian.com/music/2019/jul/19/disco-demolition-the-night-they-tried-to-crush-black-music).

13. Weisbard. *Top 40 Democracy*, pp. 28–69.

14. Wawzenek, Bryan. "Top Ten Classic Rock Disco Songs," Ultimate Classic Rock, February 12, 2014 (ultimateclassicrock.com/classic-rock-disco-songs).

15. Peck. *Rolling Stone*, pp. 8–16.

16. George, Nelson. *The Death of Rhythm and Blues* (Penguin Books, 1988), p. 181.

17. Peck. *Rolling Stone*, pp. 8–16.

18. Tschmuck, Peter. "The Recession in the Music Industry—A Cause Analysis," *Music Business Research*, March 29, 2010 (musicbusinessresearch.wordpress.com/2010/03/29/the-recession-in-the-music-industry-a-cause-analysis).

19. George. *The Death of Rhythm and Blues*, pp. 150–82.

20. George. *The Death of Rhythm and Blues*.

21. George. *The Death of Rhythm and Blues.*

22. George. *The Death of Rhythm and Blues.*

23. George. *The Death of Rhythm and Blues.*

24. Berns, Brett and Sarles, Bob. "Bang! The Burt Berns Story," 2016 (HCTN, Ravin' Films).

25. Taysom, John. "John Lennon Defends the Beatles 'Ripping Off' Black Music in a Handwritten Note," *Far Out Magazine*, November 6, 2020 (faroutmagazine.co.uk/john-lennon-defends-beatles-ripping-off-black-musicians-in-a-handwritten-note).

26. Weisbard. *Top 40 Democracy*, pp. 28–69.

Chapter 6

1. Orpheus, Rodney. "The Economics of the Music Industry and the Impact of Digital Technology," *Medium*, May 8, 2017 (rodneyorpheus.medium.com/the-digital-music-industry-an-overview).

   Yetnikoff, Walter and Ritz, David. *Howling at the Moon: The Odyssey of a Monstrous Music Mogul in an Age of Excess* (Broadway Books, 2004), p. 69.

2. Dannen, Frederic. *Hit Men* (Vintage Books, First Edition, 1991 (Random House)), pp. 18–19.

3. Dannen. *Hit Men.*

4. Yetnikoff and Ritz. *Howling at the Moon*, p. 90.

5. Dannen. *Hit Men*, pp. 18–19.

6. Yetnikoff and Ritz. *Howling at the Moon*, p. 256.

7. Sigerson, Davitt. "Ernie Isley: Pride of the Isleys," *Black Music*, September 1977 (rocksbackpages.com/Library/Article/ernie-isley-pride-of-the-isleys).

8. Yetnikoff and Ritz. *Howling at the Moon*, p. 90.

9. Mimbs Nyce, Caroline. "When CDs Launched in America," *The Atlantic*, March 2, 2016 (theatlantic.com/technology/archive/2016/03/march-1983-cds-launch-in-america).

10. Philips, Chuck. "HOME ENTERTAINMENT: High Cost of Listening: CDs Rejuvenated Album Sales in the 80s, but Business Is Declining Again and Retailers Say That's Because the Labels Won't Cut Prices," *Los Angeles Times* (Entertainment & Arts), May 3, 1992 (latimes.com/archives/la-xpm-1992-05-03-ca-2007-story.html).

11. Zepeda, Rebeca. "Changing the Business: Music Videos in Society," *Backstage Pass*, Vol. 1, Issue no. 1, Article 19 (2018), pp. 5–10 (scholarlycommons.pacific.edu/backstage-pass/vol1/iss1/19).

12. Zepeda. "Changing the Business: Music Videos in Society."

13. Hervey II, Ramon. "When Rick James Fought to Get Black Artists on MTV," *Literary Hub,* August 19, 2022 (https://lithub.com/when-rick-james-fought-to-get-black-artists-on-mtv).

14. Weisbard, Eric. *Top 40 Democracy: The Rival Mainstreams of American Music* (The University of Chicago Press, 2014), pp. 28–69.

15. Yetnikoff and Ritz. *Howling at the Moon*, pp. 154–5.

16. Mitchell, Gail. "How Michael Jackson's 'Thriller' Changed the Music Business," *Billboard*, July 3, 2009 (billboard.com/music/music-news/exclusive-how-michael-jacksons-thriller-changed-the-music-business).

17. George, Nelson. *The Death of Rhythm and Blues* (Penguin Books, 1988), pp. 147–56.

18. Knox, Ron. "Big Music Needs to Be Broken up to Save the Industry," *WIRED,* March 12, 2011 (https://www.wired.com/

story/opinion-big-music-needs-to-be-broken-up-to-save-the-industry).

19. Sigerson. "Ernie Isley: Pride of the Isleys."

20. George. *The Death of Rhythm and Blues*, pp. 179–83.

21. Uncredited., "IRS after Isley Bros.; NJ Mansion Has Seizure Signs," *Jet Magazine*, September 13, 1979.

22. Reilly, Peter J. "An Isley Brother in Tax Court," *Forbes*, November 10, 2013 (forbes.com/sites/peterjreilly/2013/11/10/an-isley-brother-in-tax-court-does-tax-crime-pay).

23. Goldfine, Scott. "Quick Takes—Chris Jasper on Why the Isley Brothers Broke Up," *Truth in Rhythm*, YouTube Interview Show (youtube.com/watch?v=4MUbwXGVihk).

24. Hunt, Dennis. "Isley Brothers 'Sailin' Back on the Charts," *Los Angeles Times*, July 3, 1987 (https://www.latimes.com/archives/la-xpm-1987-07-03-ca-975-story.html).

25. Sexton, Paul. "Isley Jasper Isley: 3 Go Wild between the Sheets," *Record Mirror*, December 7, 1985 (rocksbackpages.com/Library/Article/isley- jasper-isley-3-go-wild-between-the-sheets).

26. Hunt, *Los Angeles Times*.

27. Hunt, *Los Angeles Times*.

Chapter 7

1. Weisbard, Eric. *Top 40 Democracy: The Rival Mainstreams of American Music* (The University of Chicago Press, 2014), p. 30.

2. Hamilton, Jack. *Just around Midnight: Rock and Roll and the Racial Imagination* (Harvard University Press, September 26, 2016), p. 11.

3. Pearson Higher Education, "The Blues, Rock and Roll, and Racism (Chapter 1)," (pearsonhighered.com/assets/samplechapter/0/2/0/5/0205936245.pdf).

4. Ahmed, Insanul. "Is Hip Hop's Dominance Slipping?" *Billboard Pro*, October 18, 2022 (billboard.com/pro/hip-hop-music-most-popular-genre-dominance-slipping).

5. Garafalo, Reebee. "Crossing Over: From Black Rhythm & Blues to White Rock 'N' Roll," *Rhythm and Business: The Political Economy of Black Music* (Akashit Books, 2002), pp. 112–37.

6. Dannen, Frederic. *Hit Men* (Vintage Books, First Edition, 1991 (Random House)), pp. 18–19.

7. Crowe, Charles. "Black Culture and White Power: Notes on the History of Historical Perceptions," *The Georgia Historical Quarterly*, Vol. 73, Issue 2 (Summer 1989), Georgia Historical Society, pp. 250–77.

8. Crowe, Charles. "Black Culture and White Power."

9. Mahon, Maureen. "Music, Power, Practice," *Ethnomusicology*, Vol. 58, No. 2 (Spring/Summer 2014), University of Illinois Press, pp. 327–33.

10. Pearson Higher Education, "The Blues, Rock and Roll, and Racism (Chapter 1)."

11. Dannen, Frederic. *Hit Men* (Vintage Books, First Edition, 1991 (Random House)), pp. 18–19.

12. Pearson Higher Education, "The Blues, Rock and Roll, and Racism (Chapter 1)."

13. Pearson Higher Education, "The Blues, Rock and Roll, and Racism (Chapter 1)."

14. Pearson Higher Education, "The Blues, Rock and Roll, and Racism (Chapter 1)."

15. Pearson Higher Education, "The Blues, Rock and Roll, and Racism (Chapter 1)."

16. Bangs, Lester. "White Noise Supremacists," *Village Voice*, April 30, 1979 (villagevoice.com/the-white-noise-supremacists).

Also Available in the Series

ALSO AVAILABLE IN THE SERIES

ICONS OF STYLE
Diana

The story of a fashion legend

Glenys Johnson

WELBECK

CHAPTER 3

The Key Pieces

140

CHAPTER 4

Her Legacy

186

"I like to be a free spirit.

Some don't like that, but that's the way I am."

PRINCESS DIANA

Introduction

Burned into the memories of many of those who were glued to their TV sets to witness the event, the speech given by Diana Spencer's younger brother at her funeral on 6 September 1997 gave us a line that summed up her character perfectly. "Diana was the very essence of compassion, of duty, of style, of beauty. All over the world she was a symbol of selfless humanity."

Though she was in many ways a divisive figure in her lifetime, Diana, Princess of Wales, remains an icon. The word befits her charm, her philanthropic work, her playful approach to motherhood – and her fashion sense.

But what makes somebody an icon? It's a word thrown around too freely in this age of social media exaggeration. To be iconic is to be idolized in life – and in death. It's to be known by your first name alone. It's to be not merely representative of one era but to live on as an eternal memory, remaining relevant in future decades. Many of Diana's biggest fans didn't witness the frenzy she created while she was alive, but they'll continue to find new reasons to fall in love with her and refresh her legacy in new ways.

Diana attends an event in Italy sporting crystal heart earrings by Butler & Wilson and a silk suit by Bruce Oldfield, 1985.

"Only do what your heart tells you."

Diana's outfits have come to represent far more than she could ever have imagined. Even media commentators of the eighties and nineties, who were obsessed with her, could not have predicted her current rebirth across social media. Millennials, just old enough to remember her, and Gen Zers, many born after her death, bring a whole new level of analysis and imitation to her most famous looks.

Diana's story is the haunting tale of a princess who came to a tragic end. The public will never have all the answers, but for each new generation there's an allure in shaping our own interpretation of her story. Once the most photographed woman alive, she leaves behind a documentary legacy unmatched by anyone before her. At the touch of a button or the turn of a page, it's ours to analyze: the messages contained in her fashion choices and the magic of the threads that were woven to create a wardrobe unlike any other.

Diana wears one of her trademark pieces of jewellery, an emerald choker, to the Newport International Competition for Young Pianists in 1985.

Style

CHAPTER 1

Trajectory

The evolution
of a wardrobe

Born Diana Spencer on 1 July 1961 to parents John Spencer and Frances Shand Kydd, Lady Diana would go on to become one of the most famous faces of the twentieth century. Her rise to fame began with her marriage to Charles III, then the Prince of Wales, but many would forever remember her for her charm and her unshakable kindness. And alongside her philanthropy and her dedication to making the world a better place, her wardrobe would always shine bright.

From the frill collars of the eighties to the mini dresses of the nineties, Diana's inspirational life of independence and charitable deeds was accompanied by outfits that always told a story. Now, decades later, her legacy lives on through the modern-day It girls, pop stars and leading actresses who continue to reference Diana's daring looks both on and off the red carpet.

What did it take for this somewhat shy, affectionate child to become the most famous woman in the world? Many pages and many words have gone into tracing this lineage, drawing a thousand conclusions. But what if the clothes signalled more than anyone who was watching thought? Observe Diana's evolution from preppy Sloane Ranger to world-famous femme fatale and draw your own conclusions.

A teenage Diana is captured by photographer Arthur Edwards on a break from her duties at a nursery in Pimlico, 1980.

Sloane Ranger

The early eighties was an unforgettable time for fashion. In New York there were the hip-hop crews in their baggy clothes and sportswear ensembles. London was inhabited by an eclectic mix of leather-clad punks, New Romantics (defined by their stark make-up, larger-than-life hair and Gothic style) and, most importantly (for this book, anyway), Sloane Rangers.

A unique, British approach to what many Americans would define as the "preppy" look, the Sloane Ranger style was embodied and defined by the upper-middle-class youth who lived near Sloane Square, in the London district of Kensington. Amid a sea of Barbour jackets, corduroy trousers and flowing pleated skirts, we meet the shy 19-year-old Diana Spencer. Diana was to bring the Sloane Ranger style to the international stage – but at the time, her look was very much a drop in the bucket, simply the uniform that everyone wore. It signalled that she belonged to a particular class. The Sloane wardrobe was said to have been influenced by a traditionally minded lifestyle which took in weekends at the family home in the country and weekday glasses of red at one of the higher-end drinking holes in the area. The Fulham pub The White Horse, known to locals as the Sloaney Pony, was full of Sloane Ranger types throughout the early eighties.

Diana's role in bringing Sloane Ranger style to the masses is highlighted by her cover spot on *The Official Sloane Ranger Handbook*, released in 1982, two years after the release of *The Official Preppy Handbook*, which defined the Sloane's

ABOVE A young Diana is captured by paparazzi in Kensington
amid rumours that she is dating Prince Charles, 1980.

OVERLEAF Posing a contrast to the Sloane Rangers were the New
Romantics, pictured here on Chelsea's King's Road, 1980.

> "When Diana Spencer began to appear in newspapers in the summer of 1980, the *Sloane Ranger* style began its gallop down to the high streets."

THE OFFICIAL SLOANE RANGER HANDBOOK

A typical Sloane couple, here attending a horse race in Liverpool, 1985.

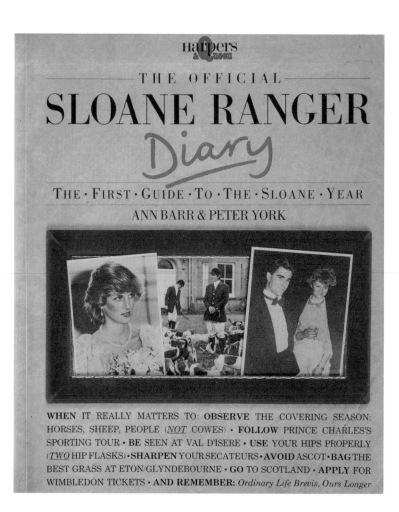

THE OFFICIAL

SLOANE RANGER
Diary

THE · FIRST · GUIDE · TO · THE · SLOANE · YEAR

ANN BARR & PETER YORK

WHEN IT REALLY MATTERS TO: **OBSERVE** THE COVERING SEASON: HORSES, SHEEP, PEOPLE (*NOT* COWES) • **FOLLOW** PRINCE CHARLES'S SPORTING TOUR • **BE SEEN AT VAL D'ISERE** • **USE** YOUR HIPS PROPERLY (*TWO* HIP FLASKS) • **SHARPEN** YOUR SECATEURS • **AVOID** ASCOT • **BAG** THE BEST GRASS AT ETON/GLYNDEBOURNE • **GO TO SCOTLAND** • **APPLY** FOR WIMBLEDON TICKETS • **AND REMEMBER:** *Ordinary Life Brevis, Ours Longer*

The Official Sloane Ranger Handbook inspired books like The Official Sloane Ranger Diary, with Diana appearing on the cover.

American counterpart. Both books took a satirical look at the style-focused communities and their seemingly endless list of insider rules – from the forms of transport that were acceptable (Diana drove a modest Volvo when she started dating Charles, a vehicle embraced by the Sloanes as robust and practical) to the alcoholic drink choices that were celebrated. The handbook was followed up with *The Official Sloane Ranger Diary* in 1983, Diana again gracing the cover.

Peter York, co-author of *The Official Sloane Ranger Handbook*, explains the phenomenon best. In a 2001 article for the *Guardian*, he stated, "The Sloane was a whole social phenomenon in the mid-eighties, really about upper-middle-class social conventions and styles. It was not a life of the mind, but you knew where you were."

Feminine floral dresses from Laura Ashley, timeless waxed-cotton jackets from Barbour and tweed styles from Bill Pashley filled the wardrobes of the twenty-somethings, which also contained small hints of luxury from brands like Burberry and Chanel. Dressing "sensibly" was a key element of the Sloane Ranger aesthetic. Though the influence of modern fashion was evident, the core of their uniform would never steer too far from traditional, old-money styles. Oversized cotton jumpers would be paired with a pleated floral midi skirt and Chanel flats. Knitwear was handed down from mother.

Some of the earliest photographs of Diana, from the early 1980s, demonstrate the young aristocrat's firm stance as a true Sloane Ranger, sporting knitwear paired with breezy skirts and simple flats. Details were key to finishing off the look: pearls and simple gold-tone jewellery added an angelic touch. A feathered shag haircut and minimal make-up followed Diana through the earlier part of the decade. She didn't reach for a curling iron or lipstick until she began to receive invites to high-profile events.

One of the first public images captured of Diana made the headlines and had people across the globe analyzing her fashion choices: a trend that would continue throughout her life. Diana was just 19 years old when royal photographer Arthur Edwards paid her a visit at her workplace, Young England Kindergarten in London's Pimlico. The story goes that Diana's white skirt displayed a silhouette of her legs because of the angle of the sun.

"Everybody doesn't believe this, but it is the gospel truth – halfway through, the sun came out," Edwards told *Today.com* in 2017, denying that the shots were planned on purpose or intended to embarrass the young kindergarten assistant. Diana felt the impact of the press attention and according to rumours, told Charles that she "didn't want to be known as the girlfriend who had no petticoat". It's safe to say that the photo shoot was quickly overshadowed by Diana's other headline-making moments.

The wholesome, soft-spoken and down-to-earth Diana was the perfect poster child for the Sloane Ranger look and lifestyle. But Diana's simple life would be rapidly turned upside down as her relationship with Charles developed and she went from Diana Spencer, the Sloaney kindergarten worker, to the Princess of Wales, role model to young women across the world, philanthropist and mother of two. With her new title came a style evolution witnessed by fans who couldn't wait to see what looks she'd wear next.

ABOVE Diana tends to two children who attended the nursery where she worked. This shot would be the first of countless images to secure her a headline spot in the papers.

OVERLEAF Wearing the Sloane Ranger uniform with pride, Diana is captured by photographers outside her flat in November 1980.

Princess

As Diana prepared for the official photo shoot that would announce her engagement to Prince Charles, she popped into a Knightsbridge boutique, Bellville Sassoon, to find the perfect outfit for the occasion. After all, the image would likely be plastered across tea towels and commemorative plates around the world. No pressure. As she browsed the racks for inspiration, one of the shop assistants, who didn't recognize Diana, informed her that the shop was about to close and recommended that she head to Harrods, around the corner. When they discovered what had happened, the duo of designers behind the label, Belinda Bellville and David Sassoon, quickly called Diana to apologize and welcomed her back to the store. This led to a longstanding relationship with the designers, who would go on to make countless outfits for Diana, including some of her most iconic styles. The charming anecdote highlights the extent of the transformation on which Diana had embarked and the way her world was swiftly changing around her.

In 1981, after just 13 meetings between the couple, Diana's engagement to Prince Charles was announced. Accompanying the announcement came an interview and photo shoot, resulting in images that are now familiar across the globe. Diana looks bashful in a royal blue skirt suit, perhaps chosen to match her sapphire engagement ring or to signify her

Diana wears a royal blue two-piece outfit from Cojana –
a perfect match for her sapphire engagement ring, 1981.

"You could see her go from Shy Di, looking down, to becoming stronger – which she had to do."

ANWAR HUSSEIN

ascension to the royal household. Though it might not have been the first choice of garment for an eighties teen, a patterned pussy-bow blouse endowed Diana with a gravitas far beyond her years – perhaps to subtly emphasize that she was a good match for her fiancé, who was 12 years her senior.

However, the expression on Diana's face immediately betrayed her youth. The couple's somewhat stiff, uncomfortable appearance may have been due to Diana's unease in her formal clothing, her ineptitude in front of the cameras or the couple's lack of familiarity. However, the young bride later offered another explanation for the awkwardness that had been captured on film. In her 1992 memoir, Diana reflected on the moment when, in response to a reporter asking, "Are you in love?" she had answered, "Yes", and Charles, "Whatever 'love' means."

Photographed on a 1981 visit to Balmoral, Diana sports a hot pink Peruvian-style jumper that would spark countless knock-offs for decades to come.

May 1981 marked an important step on her journey to royalty. Charles invited the young Diana to Balmoral Castle in Scotland, one of Queen Elizabeth II's favourite haunts. It's reported that Diana arrived with just a small suitcase for the weekend, which is said to have caused some alarm to those present. Diana may have been perceived as out of her depth, ill prepared for a visit with the Queen of England. Despite this, Diana passed the "meet-the-family" test, and the pair were married a few months later. One of the most famous photographs from the Balmoral trip shows the young Diana in a bright pink patterned jumper, corduroy trousers and Wellington boots from Hunter. These innocent yet confident choices suggest that the prospect of becoming a royal wouldn't phase the young woman.

The costume director of *The Crown*, Amy Roberts, told the *Financial Times* in November 2020, "[Diana] got a lot of grief when she was engaged and went to the palace, people complained [that it was a constant succession of] new outfit, new outfit. And she said, I had to, I didn't have anything. She was going from a teenager into this extraordinarily rarefied world that she wasn't cut out for."

On 29 July 1981, Lady Diana Spencer became Princess Diana, marrying Prince Charles in a ceremony at Westminster Abbey, a spectacle witnessed by a staggering 750 million people around the globe. The dress became an instant symbol of Diana's coming of age, and marked the beginning of a new era in her fashion story.

Diana worked with design duo Elizabeth and David Emanuel to create her show-stopping wedding dress, pictured here on the big day in 1981.

Eleri Lynn, the curator behind the 2018 exhibition *Diana: Her Fashion Story*, told the *Independent* in 2021, "With rolling news, tabloid journalism, and the dawn of the digital age, Diana had to quickly learn the rules of royal dressing, and so the effect of Diana's wardrobe on wider public trends was much more immediate than ever before."

Being pregnant with an heir to the throne wouldn't stop Diana from having fun with her attire throughout 1982. Her maternity style ranged from a now-coveted koala-patterned knitted jumper and corduroy trousers, worn to a polo match in Windsor, to a scarlet chiffon maternity gown by David Sassoon that captivated onlookers at the Barbican Centre on a visit a few months before the princess gave birth to her son William.

The next few years would see Diana becoming more playful with her style, whether by mimicking the colours of the Canadian flag in an outfit worn to an event in Edmonton, Alberta (fun fact – Diana's birthday is the same day as Canada Day), or a stunning one-shoulder dress designed by Bruce Oldfield, which featured a circle print and ruffles.

Maternity style never looked so good. Diana wears a David Sassoon gown while pregnant with William, 1982.

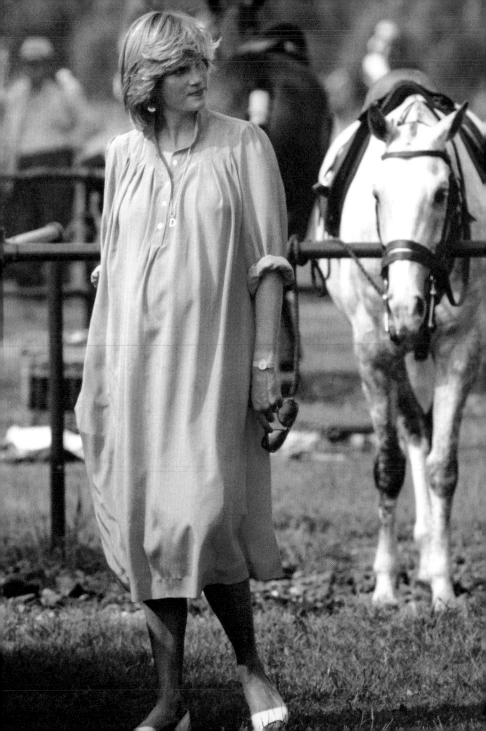

"*It was SO different from today's standard minimalist, fitted maternity wear. Instead, she leaned into trends and really went for it.*"

VOGUE'S EXECUTIVE FASHION DIRECTOR, RICKIE DE SOLE

Diana keeps things casual in a pink shirt-dress look while attending a polo match in 1982.

By 1983, Diana was venturing even further from her humble knitwear-clad days, into a world of extravagant styles that brought serious sartorial energy to the black-tie affairs she and Prince Charles frequented. The woman that the press once referred to as Shy Di due to her meek and naive persona would now be seen as Dynasty Di, a nickname nodding to the hit American TV programme starring Joan Collins and filled with bold colours, ultra sheen fabrics and larger-than-life silhouettes. It was during this period that Charles and Diana undertook a royal tour to Australia, zigzagging around the country and displaying the biggest smiles that the press would ever capture over the course of their marriage. Diana's popularity was hitting new heights – and her shoulder pads were following suit.

In 1989, the princess ventured across the pond on a solo trip, reportedly intended to "promote British industries abroad". (The increasing friction between her and Prince Charles must have provided further motivation to set off alone.) Her three-day tour of New York was an opportunity for her to solidify her role as a style icon – not just in the UK but also internationally. But while the shopping districts and boutiques of Manhattan anxiously prepared for a potential royal visit, Diana proved more interested in participating in philanthropic activities on her trip to the Big Apple. As the American press speculated about which clothing shops Diana would enter, it was clear that she was becoming known for something other than her royal status – or her charity work.

Reinterpreting the Canadian flag, Diana wears a scarlet outfit with statement collar and matching hat during a royal tour of Canada in 1983.

OPPOSITE Early in her pregnancy with William, Diana sports a pink sailor-style dress to attend the wedding of a friend in London, 1982.

ABOVE Diana attends a charity event at Barnardo's, where she chats with Joan Collins and designer friend Bruce Oldfield, 1985.

"It is said she was more beautiful in the flesh. Once, on a visit to Vogue, the art department, who'd been quite cynical about her, were agog. She had sparkle. It was simply magnetic and, in the end, it transcended her clothes."

ANNA HARVEY, *VOGUE*

Diana's right-hand women

Diana was to become known for her individuality and desire to do things her own way. But when it came to fashion, she wouldn't have been able to advance from Sloane Ranger to one of the most admired fashion icons of her time without a little help. That's where Anna Harvey came in. First crossing paths in 1980, the editor of British *Vogue* and the Princess of Wales were to form an unbreakable relationship that would continue until Diana's final days. It was Anna who introduced Diana to designers who would go on to become her favourites, including Catherine Walker, the French-born designer who many believe was Diana's sole dresser in her later years.

On Walker's passing in 2010, Anna Harvey told *Vogue*, "What Catherine did was take a girl who was essentially a Sloane Ranger before her marriage, and design for her in a straightforward, streamlined, beautiful way, with consideration of all the royal occasions."

Diana's relationships with her favourite designers were rumoured to be some of the closest she had. Bruce Oldfield, Gianni Versace, David Sassoon, Jacques Azagury and Elizabeth and David Emanuel have all spoken about their time working with her. Remembering one of their first meetings, David Emanuel recalled, "[Diana was] the most beautiful woman, inside and out. It [wasn't] just the look and the frocks and the fashion. She genuinely was

just sweet. She was very young." Catherine Walker loyally denied any and all opportunities to speak about Diana to the press.

Many of these fashion designers offered Diana an escape from her increasingly overwhelming life in the public eye, and each one helped her blossom into an icon.

"I thought she was a bit lost. But she soon became entirely empowered through fashion. It gave her a stay, and an armour, to mask a sadness. I think an enormous chasm opened up between the girl hidden inside and the different woman she had to create and present to the world," designer Arabella Pollen told *Vogue* in 2017.

Another important name in Diana's style journey was Liz Tilberis. The two met when the editor worked at British *Vogue* and Diana was first delving into the fashion world. Tilberis would go on to become editor-in-chief of *Harper's Bazaar*. The friendship is said to have become closest in the final decade of Diana's life, when her relationship with Charles was coming to an end and Tilberis was undergoing chemotherapy for ovarian cancer. It was alongside Tilberis that Diana would attend the Met Gala in 1996, wearing one of her most famous looks.

ABOVE Diana reviews fabric swatches with designer duo the Emanuels in 1986. The pair designed some of Diana's most iconic looks, including her wedding dress.

PREVIOUS Long-time friends and collaborators Diana Spencer and Catherine Walker pose with a dress at Kensington Palace, 1993.

ABOVE David Sassoon was known to be one of Diana's favourite
designers. The two are pictured here at a charity event in 1997.

RIGHT One of the rumoured 70 sketches that David Sassoon
made for Diana when designing outfits for the princess.

Independence

Diana was known to play with both official and unspoken sartorial rules while married to Prince Charles. Once their relationship ended, the rule book was thrown away completely. As the nineties pushed many fashionistas into new realms of experimentation, using garments as a means of self-expression, Diana's wardrobe too became a hotbed of messaging around her newfound independence.

"She had turned into a woman who was quite assured in her work. Who was brave and headstrong," says Jasper Conran. "The simpering princess had gone. She was not playing a part anymore. She'd found a role."

But it wasn't just her outfits that helped her explore her autonomy. Her hairstyle also played a key role in her transformation. When asked about a moment in her life when she went from "victim to victor", Diana explained that an impromptu haircut in 1991 by Sam Knight changed the game. "I suppose last summer when Sam cut my hair differently," she said, "it let out something quite different." Though it would be another couple of years before the royal couple would announce their separation, many recall the period following the haircut as a time when Diana began to move into a new era of confidence and self-assurance.

"She had turned into a woman who was quite assured in her work. Who was *brave* and *headstrong* ... The simpering princess had gone. She was not playing a part any more. She'd found a role."

JASPER CONRAN

Diana steps out confidently in a turquoise silk dress by Versace, 1996.

Diana and Charles separated in 1992 and went on to divorce in 1996. In the UK, 1992 and 1993 saw the highest rate of divorce there had ever been before – or has been recorded since. High-profile couples, from Princess Anne and Mark Phillips to Hollywood royalty Johnny Depp and Winona Ryder, were calling it quits (OK, the latter weren't actually married but for many teens of the time, they were the only couple who really mattered). It was a time when many women were experiencing a buzzing energy and a powerful sense of, well, being able to do whatever they bloody wanted. And that included breaking all the style rules.

Drag queen, performer and fashion personality Bimini said of the royal, "I feel like as Diana got more comfortable and confident in the public eye, she really knew that she was able to use the way she dressed to make a statement without having to outwardly say anything. It wasn't about being outrageous. She wasn't walking around with a lantern on her head but she would always wear something and be a bit daring and she used it to be a bit provocative. She was a cheeky lady, Diana. And she knew how to push the establishment's terms, and the media, and use it to her advantage."

At this time, Diana embraced the dramatic contrast between glamorous high-fashion style and off-duty jeans and sweats. Her red-carpet styles shone brightly with extravagant diamonds and pearls, her hemlines were shorter than she would have dared to wear before and her skinny shoulder straps were the height of fashion. She proudly sported styles from names like Versace, Jacques Azagury and Moschino – a wardrobe that many leading actresses or pop stars of the time would gladly have adopted. The impact of royal life was

"She could walk into a room of people and make them feel as if everything was great."

ELTON JOHN

Princess Diana and Mother Teresa at the Missionaries of Charity in New York, 1997.

nowhere to be seen. Diana was relishing the chance to engage fully with all the weird and wonderful nineties trends – with her own twist applied, of course.

"She was comfortable in multiple versions of herself. I think that's also something that's common today – not wanting to be one version of yourself as a woman. You want to inherit all of them. There was definitely a power in that effortlessness," said associate costume designer and head buyer on *The Crown*, Sidonie Roberts.

When she wasn't visiting war-torn countries on humanitarian missions or at a gala to raise money for cancer research, one of Diana's favourite activities in the nineties was visiting her local gym for a good old sweat session. Arguably one her most famous looks today remains an ensemble made up of spandex cycling shorts and an oversized cotton crew-neck sweatshirt, worn to journey to and from a training session at The Harbour Club in London's Chelsea neighbourhood.

Whether it was down to a new haircut, new hobbies or a newly ditched man, Diana entered the later years of the nineties invested with an unfamiliar, hard-earned independence. She had never been an adult in the public eye without the watchful, overbearing protection of one of the most powerful institutions in history. The most famous woman on the planet was now single and the world waited with bated breath to see what her next move – and her next look – would be.

One of many Diana gym looks that continue to inspire copycats decades later, 1997.

Diana's

CHAPTER 2

Greatest Hits

Narrowing down Diana's most impactful looks over nearly 20 years in the spotlight is no easy task. Each of her outfits tells an important part of her story. Taken together, they weave a tale that combines deep sadness and electric inspiration. Often the messages she was sending through her style were considered and a conscious choice of a tactical way of using her voice without speaking, whereas other times the clues of significance would be woven by the onlookers, and often in hindsight some years later.

Elizabeth Debicki, who depicted Diana in season five of *The Crown*, commented, "It's an extraordinary thing to watch. To decide what you're saying about yourself through fashion ... it was a currency. An incredibly powerful currency."

The royal years

Diana's days as HRH Princess of Wales were a rollercoaster of highs and lows, as she struggled to navigate media scrutiny, motherhood and royal practices. While most twenty-somethings were furthering their careers and beginning to consider marriage and parenting, Diana was having to navigate royalty and parenthood in front of a global audience – and the press weren't being very forgiving. As she began to come into her own, so did her sense of style. What began as a dedication to ultra-feminine gowns, florals and flouncy fabrics shifted into a love of sharp tailoring, high-fashion frocks and playful

Diana wears a polka-dot dress by Donald Campbell and a John Boyd hat on a visit to Perth, Australia, in 1983.

"So many people supported me through my public life and I will never forget them."

PRINCESS DIANA

An angelic Diana poses for a portrait wearing a frill-collar top and pearl earrings, 1983.

androgyny. Whenever Diana stepped out at an event or went on a school run, the world scrutinized her outfit and took every opportunity to dissect its meaning.

Proving that she could fuse princess elegance (that fascinator) with on-trend looks (the eighties were liberally sprinkled with polka dots), Diana stepped out to visit the Fremantle Hospital in Perth, Australia, on a royal tour that demonstrated serious style. The dress, created by Canadian fashion designer Donald Campbell, featured a soft silhouette with puff shoulders, a curved hem and a gathered waist. The accessories included a simple white clutch and a pillbox hat with statement bow designed by the respected British milliner John Boyd.

Catherine Walker does what she does best in the design of this totally timeless blazer dress, worn by Diana at a naval base in La Spezia during the royal tour of Italy in 1985. The pinstripe style features a double-breasted fastening and an exaggerated lapel – because why not? But arguably the best part of this outfit is the Kangol hat. The cult British brand would go on to cover the heads of basically every celeb throughout the nineties and early two thousands with its bucket hats and flat caps, which featured that famous kangaroo logo. Seems like the logo didn't make it onto Diana's hat, but it's definitely proof that she was ahead of her time.

Catherine Walker gets the credit for this double-breasted number, styled here with a Kangol hat on a royal tour of Italy, 1985.

OPPOSITE During the Royal Tour of Italy in 1985, Diana wears
a Catherine Walker dress and hat by John Boyd.

ABOVE Diana works a military look in a Catherine Walker dress
while visiting Sandhurst Military Academy, 1987.

"*I don't go by the rule book.*"

PRINCESS DIANA

A black and yellow coat by Escada and a Philip Somerville hat
help Diana shine on a visit to the Isle of Wight, 1988.

Was Diana the first devotee of dopamine dressing? She might well have been. Anyone's mood would be lifted by the striking pairing of hot pink and red in this Catherine Walker design, which Diana wore on a visit to Abu Dhabi, United Arab Emirates, in March 1989. The look was styled with a wide-brimmed hat made by Philip Somerville. The royals' favourite milliner created a pink ribbon that wrapped around the design, fastened with a gold pin, to match the dress perfectly. This look completely flouted fashion's unwritten rule that pink and red should never be paired.

Over 30 years on, we still see the former fashion *faux pas* standing the test of time, as names like Giambattista Valli, Rick Owens and New York designer Mara Hoffman demonstrate their obsession with the colours in their recent collections. Mara Hoffman has even managed to fuse two of Diana's most brilliant fashion legacies – the pairing of red and pink and the tank dress – into one item with her Sloan Dress (a play on Sloane, as in Sloane Ranger? Maybe).

Diana ditches outdated fashion rules in a red and pink Catherine Walker dress and statement hat by Philip Somerville in Abu Dhabi, 1989.

OPPOSITE A turban hat by Philip Somerville got the nod of approval from fashion lovers across the globe when Diana wore it alongside a Catherine Walker design during her visit to the Middle East in 1989.

ABOVE Diana looked to Italian fashion house Moschino for this olive-green two-piece outfit worn on a trip to Tokyo in 1990.

"*I knew what my job was; it was to go out and meet the people and love them.*"

PRINCESS DIANA

For the first Christmas after her separation from Charles, Diana wore a striking red coat, black dress and a black hat complete with a veil. This look would become the inspiration for one of the key ensembles worn by Kristen Stewart in the 2021 film *Spencer*.

Glamour

Before she found herself married to an actual prince, Diana Spencer's opportunities to sport lavish gowns and diamond-studded, floor-grazing dresses were pretty slim. As she gained comfort and confidence in the public eye, the glamorous looks became more commonplace in her ever-growing wardrobe. The details of Diana's most eye-catching looks would become key signifiers in the story of her life, through her coming of age, womanhood and motherhood, and later, as she found true independence as a confident single woman. Here we explore some of those key looks and their significance.

Imagine your chosen date outfit causing such a stir that the UK government had to postpone announcing the budget for the year because the press was having a field day. That's the kind of impact Diana made on the media in 1981, before she had even married Prince Charles. It was the couple's first official engagement together, a trip to a charity gala concert at the Goldsmiths' Hall, and understandably, Diana wanted to look her best. She had approached designers Elizabeth and David Emanuel to create a gown made of pastel-hued netting that aligned with her angelic look at the time. But the story goes that when Diana spotted a strapless black number on the rail of the designer duo's Brook Street showroom,

Diana hit the headlines in this black gown by David and Elizabeth Emanuel, worn on the young couple's first official outing in 1981.

Elizabeth Emanuel proudly presents the gown that would go down in history as one of Diana's most iconic looks. The design sold for nearly £200,000 at an auction in 2010.

the plan of arriving pretty in pink was quickly forgotten. It's likely that, with her limited experience in the limelight, she would have been unaware of the impact this dress would have, not only on the press and avid onlookers of the time, but on fashion history.

The taffeta style showed off Diana's slender shoulders and featured a sweetheart neckline with frills as far as the eye could see. The royals are known for their strict dress codes – one being that black is reserved for periods of mourning. Though quiet and shy, Diana dressed as she pleased that evening. It was an early hint of the rebellious approach she would take in years to come. For many, this moment took Diana Spencer to fashion icon overnight. And we can see why.

On 29 July 1981, Diana Spencer became Diana, Princess of Wales. Such an occasion would call for a wedding dress unlike any other. It's rumoured that hundreds if not thousands of pitches arrived at the palace as designers bid for a chance to design the dress that the world would admire on that summer's day. But for Diana, the choice was obvious.

Diana had collaborated with the Emanuels on a number of head-turning styles already and she was keen to continue their working relationship. The next piece she commissioned from them would change their lives completely.

"It happened out of the blue. She rang my studio and said, 'Would you do the honour of designing my wedding gown?'" David Emanuel recalls. Work quickly began on a dress that would impress a staggering audience, 750 million people, who would tune in to watch the wedding from across the globe.

One of the closest-guarded designs in fashion history, the dress Diana Spencer wore to wed Prince Charles on 29 July 1981 was a tour de force. Featuring multiple romantic details, it conjured up the essence of the fairy tale that Diana had been promised her life would become.

The brief for the dress was, well, non-existent. Elizabeth Emanuel told *People* magazine in 2018, "[Diana] was just lovely, really kind of easy going. We never had any special instructions about how to make the wedding dress. That added a bit to the fun of it all, made it bit of an adventure."

The stunning silk gown featured a ruffled collar, puffed sleeves (ever popular in the eighties), a voluminous skirt decked with approximately 10,000 pearls and an 18-karat-gold horseshoe charm, which was secretly sewn into the body of the dress for good luck by the Emanuels. But probably the most famous feature of the dress was the 25-foot train that covered the aisle of Westminster Abbey and tulle veil that spanned 153 yards (almost 140 metres). The train continues to hold the record as the longest in royal history. Sewn into the design was antique Carrickmacross lace, which had belonged to Queen Mary (and which represented the "something old" that tradition dictates all royal brides should have in their wedding dress).

Tying the look together was a garland-style tiara, made in 1930, from diamonds belonging to the Spencer family, by famous Mayfair jeweller Garrard. Diana's mother Frances Shand Kydd lent Diana her earrings for the big day. A central pear-shaped diamond was surrounded by smaller diamonds to add extra shimmer.

Diana becomes the Princess of Wales in a dress designed by the Emanuels, 1981.

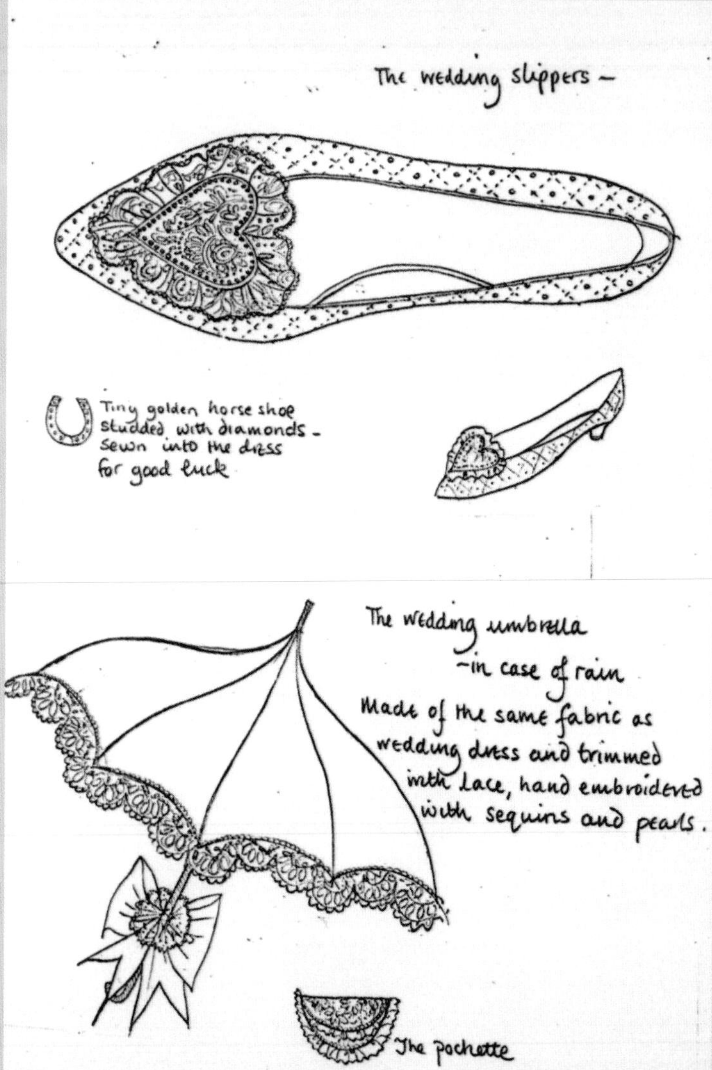

The wedding slippers —

Tiny golden horse shoe studded with diamonds - sewn into the dress for good luck.

The wedding umbrella
— in case of rain.
Made of the same fabric as wedding dress and trimmed with lace, hand embroidered with sequins and pearls.

The pochette

A sketch by the Emanuels depicting Diana's wedding shoes and a bespoke umbrella design that was to be used in case of rain on the big day.

Elizabeth Emanuel worked with renowned UK cobbler Clive Shilton on the silk satin shoes, which were covered with 542 sequins and 132 seed pearls and displaying a heart motif on the toe. The heel was kept low (to ensure Diana didn't tower over Prince Charles), a decision that *Vogue France* described as "a hymn to romance". "The gesture symbolized great tenderness and a note of naivety from a woman who did not yet know what the future held for her and the prince she loved," stated Anna Maria Giano, editor at *Vogue Italia* in an online piece in July 2022.

The dress created such a buzz in the bridal gown industry that replica designs were popping up mere hours after the wedding. Just days later, copycat styles were on display in shop windows.

Diana's beauty was captured in repose when she managed to catch a few zzzs while attending an event at the Victoria and Albert Museum in London four months after her wedding to Prince Charles. The famous photograph shows the Princess of Wales in a flowing off-the-shoulder Bellville Sassoon dress with a hand-painted pattern, satin trim and ruffled hem. Diana's pearl choker, which was becoming something of a trademark piece for the princess, was matched with a statement bracelet and matching earrings. As much as we'd love to say that this was another cheeky way to show the royals that she played by her own rules, the palace announced the next day that the 20-year-old, freshly dubbed "Sleeping Beauty" by the press, was in fact exhausted because she was in the early stages of pregnancy with Prince William.

OVERLEAF The famous dress was available for the public to inspect at *Royal Style in the Making*, an exhibit at Kensington Palace, 2022.

"*It took a long time to understand why people were so interested in me.*"

PRINCESS DIANA

"Sleeping Beauty" Diana opts for a pretty pastel Bellville Sassoon style for an outing to the Victoria and Albert Museum in London, 1981.

OPPOSITE Diana shimmers in a red Bellville Sassoon dress while
attending a ballet performance at the Royal Opera House, 1982.

ABOVE Feminine frills make this Emanuel design
pop on a visit to Claridge's Hotel, 1981.

Diana had an affinity for shimmering styles with serious eighties charm. A key example of Diana's affinity for shimmering styles with serious eighties charm, the Bruce Oldfield number (seen right) made headlines during the couple's 1983 tour of Australia. The new parents made the most of their evening at a charity gala in Sydney by dancing the night away (one of Diana's favourite pastimes).The aquamarine style featured all-over ruffles, metallic thread and a floor-length hem. A bold, metallic leather belt and heels tied things together. Lady Di was adorned in a glittering diamond necklace with matching earrings and bracelet. Recognize the look? A rendition made its way into season four of Netflix's *The Crown*.

On the final night of the six-week tour, Prince Charles and Princess Diana attended a dinner in Melbourne, Australia, where Diana presented herself in a stunning single-shoulder dress designed for her by independent Japanese couturier Hachi. The dress, which had been suggested to Diana by Anna Harvey, was made of white silk and featured silver bugle beads and medallion appliques at the gathered hip and shoulder. The dress would be one of the princess' favourites. She wore it again later the same year, for a second time in 1985 at the National Gallery in Washington, DC, and for a third time in 1989 for the London premiere of the 16th film in the 007 series, *Licence to Kill*. The dress sold at auction for $60,000 (the equivalent of around £85,000 in 2022) in June 1997, just a few months before Diana's death in August of the same year.

The Crown fans may recognise this dress: it inspired a style seen in season four. The original, seen here, was designed by Bruce Oldfield and is styled with a bold silver-tone belt and matching pumps, 1983.

"*I have a woman's instinct and it's always a good one.*"

PRINCESS DIANA

Visiting The White House in 1985, Diana wore what would become one of her most famous dresses. The navy number was created by one of Diana's favourite designers, British couturier Victor Edelstein, reputedly after Diana spotted a burgundy version in his studio. The Princess of Wales requested that Edelstein create a version for her in one of her favourite colours, midnight blue. The fitting for the dress reportedly took place at Diana's suite in Kensington Palace, where the princess was so thrilled with the result that it's said she immediately rushed off to show the style to Prince Charles.

Diana rapidly learned how to make an impact. She knew that the midnight-blue velvet dress by Victor Edelstein, which she wore when she danced with John Travolta at the White House, was one heck of a number – and it thrilled her.

A big cinema buff and music fan, the princess was honoured to meet John Travolta at The White House. The actor was known for his dancing skills, which he'd demonstrated in leading roles in films like *Saturday Night Fever* and *Grease*. It's rumoured that Mr Travolta had caught wind that the Princess of Wales was interested in dancing with him. Following a tap on the shoulder and a polite request, Diana accepted a dance to the Bee Gees' song "You Should Be Dancing".

OPPOSITE The Princess of Wales attends a gala ballet performance in Auckland, New Zealand, wearing a lilac gown by Donald Campbell, 1983.

OVERLEAF This Victor Edelstein gown would come to be known as simply the "Travolta dress", after Diana captured the attention of the world by dancing with the American actor at a White House event in 1985.

But it wasn't just the midnight-blue dress that captured the attention of onlookers that night. The princess also wore a magnificent choker featuring seven rows of pearls and a blue sapphire surrounded by shimmering diamonds. The sapphire was reported to have been given to the young princess by the Queen Mother in the form of a large oval sapphire and diamond brooch: a wedding gift to her new granddaughter-in-law. The accessory was evidence of Diana's creative flair for playing with fashion, and it became a key piece for the princess, worn for the next decade (and making an appearance alongside her "revenge dress" and 1996 Met Gala look). Wearing your ex's nan's jewellery to a high-profile event after your break-up is a serious power move.

In early 1989, Diana took a solo three-day trip to New York, an event that Netflix's *The Crown* references in season four. On her second evening in the city, she attended a gala dinner at the World Financial Center's Winter Garden wearing a Victor Edelstein gown with matching bolero. The white satin outfit was covered in beaded detailing and is said to have captivated nearly everyone in attendance.

"Since it was New York, everyone was wearing black [...] So when Diana entered the box, radiant in a magnificent long white dress with a matching bolero jacket covered in jewels, a gasp went up from the crowd," Brooks Hopkins told *People* magazine in 2020.

Diana arrives to see the Welsh National Opera Gala production of *Falstaff* wearing a pearly white dress designed by Victor Edelstein, 1989.

OPPOSITE Diana wears a red and black floral gown by Catherine Walker
to an event at the British Embassy in Paris, France, 1989.

ABOVE The "Elvis dress" by Catherine Walker helped secure Diana's spot
as one of the world's most fashionable women, seen here in 1989.

It's impossible to analyze Diana's approach to style without mentioning the "revenge dress". We can speculate at length about the significance of the looks she wore throughout her life, trying to decipher what the princess might have meant by them, but the message of this outfit arrives loud and clear.

Diana made history with her wardrobe on 29 June 1994. Prince Charles had just made headlines with his interview at Highgrove House, in which he came clean about his affair with Camilla Parker-Bowles (though the *New York Times* had leaked his revelation two days before the interview aired). That same evening, Diana attended an event hosted by *Vanity Fair* at the Serpentine Gallery in London's Hyde Park. Her striking little black dress was by Christina Stambolian, a Greek designer. It featured a figure-hugging silhouette crafted from delicate crepe with cap sleeves (which Diana wore off the shoulder), a ruched bodice and flowing black chiffon sash.

The *Telegraph* commented, "The Princess of Wales did not have to dine out before the television cameras at the Serpentine Gallery last night in order to avoid seeing her husband sharing his soul with the nation on the box. She could have watched a video, played bridge, or simply washed her hair and curled up in bed ... It's amazing what some people will do to avoid press speculation."

Diana makes fashion history in this Christina Stambolian dress, which became known as the "revenge dress", when she wears it to an event at the Serpentine Gallery in 1994.

"*I can't really explain it. It's pretty incredible that a dress would represent* a *moment in history*... *that this human's life would represent so much and* become *so iconic.*"

ELIZABETH DEBICKI

The legacy of the dress lives on. 29 June will forever be known as "revenge dress day", as highlighted by an Instagram post from the *Telegraph*'s style section on the date in 2020, reading: "Happy revenge dress day (emojis). 26 years ago Princess Diana wore her famous LBD by Greek designer Christina Stambolian to the Serpentine Gallery party (emojis). Click the link in bio for why Princess Diana's revenge dress is still relevant."

Elizabeth Debicki, the lucky Australian actor who portrayed the "People's Princess" in season five of *The Crown*, was interviewed in the press about what it was like to recreate the iconic look. "It fascinated me how entranced people were with that dress," she recalled to *Entertainment Weekly* in October 2022. "When it became known that I had the part, I received these text messages saying congratulations, [but] there was also a huge amount of text messages about the revenge dress. 'Do you get to wear the revenge dress?' 'Oh, my God, you get to wear the revenge dress!'"

Elizabeth Debicki
recreating the iconic
revenge dress
moment for season
five of *The Crown*.

"*She really loved the* world of fashion, *and she liked the people in it.* It was an escape *for her.*"

STEPHEN JONES

Appearing fresh and confident on her 36th birthday, Diana sports a shimmering floor-length dress by Jacques Azagury, 1997.

Off-duty style

Diana's high-fashion styles charmed the world, but her off-duty looks played an important role in identifying her not as just a princess, with a wardrobe most other women could only dream of, but someone who had relatable personal taste. The former princess's weekend wardrobe offered her own take on the trends of the time. She paired denim with diamonds and oversized tees with designer handbags. Her laid-back looks were beloved by audiences at the time – and they're arguably even more loved now. Let's take a peek at some of the off-the-clock looks that Diana fans can't get enough of.

One of her most talked-about looks, which spoke to Diana's Sloane Ranger origins, was her "black sheep" jumper, which she wore with blue jeans to watch Charles play in a polo match in June 1981. The jumper was from Warm & Wonderful, an independent brand which started out from a stall in London's Covent Garden market.

The duo behind the label, Sally Muir and Joanna Osborne, spoke to the *New Yorker* about the outfit in 2020. They said they didn't know how Diana obtained the jumper, but that the rumour was that it was gifted to her by the mother of one of the page boys at her wedding.

The jumper would make a second appearance a few years after the couple's marriage, this time worn with a statement collar with black ribbon, high-waisted white jeans and oversized sunglasses.

This design by Warm & Wonderful would go on to be one of Diana's most coveted knitwear looks, seen here at a polo match in 1981.

"She dressed to communicate *approachability* and *warmth* – to encourage *informality.*"

ELERI LYNN

An incredibly eighties look sported by Diana at
one of her outings to watch the polo in 1983.

OPPOSITE Another polo match outfit, this time a floral skirt and sailor blouse, 1985.

ABOVE Diana embraces the eighties ruched-waist trend
in this floral Bellville Sassoon dress, 1988.

In a 2022 documentary, *Diana: A Life in Fashion*, fashion editor Penny Goldstone speculates on the significance of the jumper. "You can very much tell that there's been a shift between the two pictures. In the second image, she's standing straighter. She's kind of looking at the camera [...] I think the first time she wore it, [she] wasn't thinking anything about it." She went on, "A lot of people were saying it was a statement at the time because there were already a few arguments with Prince Charles. She was considered a bit of a rebel, she didn't want to follow all the rules in the family so it sort of symbolized her being the 'black sheep' of the Royal Family."

It takes some serious sartorial nous to throw together a look that not only continues to inspire the fashion world over three decades later, but also raises awareness of a good cause. Well, Diana had that talent. In 1988, the 27-year-old Diana stepped out to watch the polo at Guards Polo Club in Windsor. Recreated in season five of *The Crown*, the famous look consisted of one of her favourite navy baseball caps, rumoured to have been a gift from the Royal Canadian Mounted Police, an oversized blazer, white British Lung Foundation sweatshirt, blue jeans and slouchy leather boots. The British Lung Foundation was thrilled with the attention that resulted from the princess' moment of endorsement, but it wasn't just that the jumper was comfy: Diana had become a patron of the foundation two years earlier. The crew-neck style continues to be available for purchase on the foundation's website, which refers to it as the "Diana sweatshirt".

The Princess of Wales pairs a British Lung Foundation sweatshirt with jeans, boots and a baseball cap to visit the Guards Polo Club, 1988.

ecker Island
PRIVATE
NO ENTRY
r Information call
4·2757-4·4492
Monitor Ch.16

OPPOSITE Diana's 1989 school-run outfit embodies understated elegance, pairing a striped cardigan with a pleated midi skirt and simple pumps.

ABOVE Diana knew the power of a strong animal-inspired print when it came to holiday style, 1990.

Many women will understand the importance of the perfect beach outfit for an Instagram-worthy holiday. Now imagine you're the most photographed woman in the world and your destination is Richard Branson's private island. Plus, there's a round-the-clock stakeout by photographers from some of the biggest newspapers and magazines in the world. By the looks of it, the pressure didn't get to her. Enjoying a royal family holiday, Diana made headlines with her leopard-print ensemble, which paired a classic one-piece swimming costume with a semi-sheer midi wrap skirt in the same pattern. She added sunglasses in one of her favourite shapes, the timeless Wayfarer. Jantzens, the Portland-based label behind the one-piece style, was reported to be one of Diana's favourites when it came to swimwear, as its designs suited a long torso, flattering her five-foot-ten frame. She'd go on to sport a similar style on the last holiday before her death, this time created by Israeli designer Gottex.

Double denim. A Canadian tuxedo. Whatever you call it, Princess Diana embraced the nineties' calling card while on a skiing holiday with her sons in Lech, Austria, in 1994. To many women, this look painted Diana as the perfect combination of fashion icon and approachable best friend – someone with whom you could see yourself going shopping, or sharing the *après-ski* lifestyle. The mid-wash look was punctuated with a crocodile-effect leather belt, a classic leather bomber jacket and white padded snow boots. Bonus points go to the young Prince William for those fleece-lined Moon Boots – the Y2K staple that Hailey Bieber, Iris Apatow and Dua Lipa have brought back into the limelight.

A young Prince William and Diana step out in denim, 1992.

"She was a **superstar**, she was *royal*, but she was also very **approachable.**"

TIM GRAHAM

Gold-tone details make this Wimbledon look come to life, 1993.

In the summer of 1997, Diana took a trip to Bosnia with the Landmine Survivors Network. The 36-year-old philanthropist knew this wasn't an occasion to be sporting flashy styles or making big statements with her outfits. To keep the focus on the cause, her looks would need to be pared back. She opted for a pair of light-wash, high-waisted jeans with a tapered leg (we'd identify them as Mom jeans, but they weren't called that at the time) and a classic white shirt. Ironically, for many observers, the outfits Diana wore on this trip would go on to rank among her top fashion moments, giving her an air of effortless sophistication. The jeans and shirt were accessorized with a tan leather belt, Diana's trademark driving shoes, by elegant UK label Tod's, and understated gold jewellery. Diana's minimalist late-nineties style proved that the former princess could do no wrong when it came to casual dressing.

Diana beams in a casual varsity-style jacket while on an outing to the Alton Towers theme park with Harry and William in 1994.

ABOVE Nothing beats a jeans and blazer combo, as proven by this snap of Diana shopping in Knightsbridge, 1994.

OPPOSITE Diana was known to love her Gucci bamboo-handle bag, spotted here after a trip to the gym in 1996.

OPPOSITE On her final humanitarian trip, Diana wore light-wash
jeans, a plain white shirt and her Tod's loafers, 1997.

ABOVE Diana's wardrobe for Bosnia was understated as
per the fashion for casual looks of the time.

Sport

Long before names like Gymshark and Lululemon offered the world their deluxe high-waisted leggings, made using high-tech materials with names like Luxtreme®, and boasting advanced sweat-wicking technologies that sound like they're from outer space, the world of athleisure was very different. Your options were basically cotton, nylon and Lycra® – and Diana wore them all, with a sense of style that has echoed down the decades since. In 2022, pop culture commentator Kristen Meinzer told *Newsweek*, "[Diana] was kind of the 'Princess of Athleisure' before athleisure was even called athleisure." Diana's gym outfits, oversized sweatshirts and cycling shorts, worn with dad trainers and tube socks, have heavily influenced the looks that TikTok and Instagram have obsessed over in recent years – and it's easy to see why. It's impossible not to fall in love with Diana's nonchalant style a little bit more with every look.

OPPOSITE It doesn't get more nineties than a colourful ski onesie. Diana chose a one-piece by Austrian label Kitex for a ski holiday in 1993.

OVERLEAF Diana and Sarah Ferguson prove they got the memo when it came to skiwear choice, posing here for a photo during a ski holiday in 1983.

On a 1987 trip, Diana wore one of the most eighties outfits of all time, joining some royal companions to hit the slopes at the Klosters ski resort in Switzerland. Just one of many bold snowsuits that the princess would select over the years, this one-piece features a belted waist with green and hot pink trim and a star planted in the middle of Diana's chest. In 2022, this design from Austrian label Kitex can be found on a vintage clothing site priced at a staggering £3,150. The slope-ready look is completed with mirrored aviator sunglasses and an ivory snood that screams cosy. Honourable mention is due to Fergie's wraparound sunglasses and larger-than-life hairdo.

Diana spent much of the mid- to late nineties training at one of her favourite health clubs, the Chelsea Harbour Club. It was, in some ways, an unlikely setting for the looks that decades later would become some of her most celebrated styles. We can spot her trademark oversized cotton sweatshirt and bright cycling shorts combo in the picture overleaf from 1995. Diana also wears a pair of Nike Air Max Structure trainers with snowy white Reebok sports socks. This type of look was popularized by the step aerobics trend that swept through the fitness world from the late eighties until the late nineties. Diana's navy sweatshirt was a gift from her friend Richard Branson, the founder of the Virgin brand.

Diana embraces the nineties obsession with oversized sweatshirts and cycling shorts as she leaves the Chelsea Harbour Club in 1994.

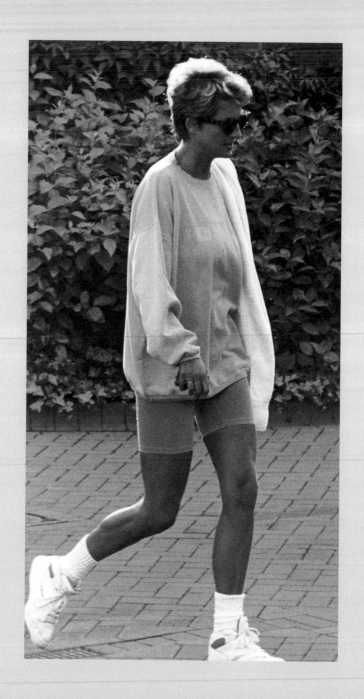

OPPOSITE The "People's Princess" wears a pale blue sweatshirt, pink shorts and tortoise-shell sunglasses, 1994.

ABOVE Diana sprints through the streets of London wearing a mock-neck Harvard sweatshirt, cycling shorts and chunky trainers, 1997.

It would become a popular piece in Diana's wardrobe of gym wear. It was reported that she wore it frequently as a way to deter paparazzi: if she dressed in the same way every day, their photos would be nearly identical and wouldn't be so in demand. Replicas of the style are still produced – and still sell out – to this day. The original sweatshirt was given to Diana's personal trainer, Jenni Rivett, in the year before Diana's death in 1997. It would go on to sell for about £48,000 at an auction in 2019.

Another TikTok and Instagram favourite is Diana's Northwestern sweatshirt, photographed after a gym session in 1996. What makes this such a good look? It's the addition of the bamboo-handled Gucci tote and tortoise-shell sunglasses. The mash-up of contrasting styles really shouldn't work – but it definitely does. The crisp white of the cycling shorts and the sweatshirt's bold font make the 35-year-old Diana's sun-kissed skin glow. The trainers are Reeboks, a nod to one of Diana's favourite sportswear brands. So, where'd the crew neck come from? Well, Diana had paid Northwestern University a visit in 1996. The academic institution is situated a short distance north of Chicago, Illinois. The purpose of the trip was to help raise awareness and funds to support the university's cancer research – a goal she achieved, raising $1.5 million (approximately £2.6 million today). Coincidentally, Meghan Markle would study theatre and international studies at Northwestern, graduating seven years after the princess' visit.

The Virgin Atlantic sweatshirt was one of Diana's favourites, worn here as she leaves her gym in Chelsea in 1995.

The Key

CHAPTER 3

Pieces

For those who are familiar with Diana's approach to fashion, a few key elements may come to mind on hearing her name. There are the accessories she managed to consistently incorporate into her outfits over nearly 20 years in the limelight and the styles that punctuated different eras of her fashion journey. Arguably, Diana even managed to claim a few colour palettes over the course of her sartorial reign. But as we know by now, it was almost never the case that Diana simply grabbed off the rack something she liked the look of – there's a story to be told about each signature piece.

Jewellery fit for a princess

The story of Diana's jewellery easily warrants a book of its own (and it has). Her love of precious pieces evolved in many ways over the years. Pretty pearls, Cartier watches and sapphires complemented many of her most popular looks, from dramatic gowns to jeans and T-shirts. The princess used jewels to ensure that her elegance was always intact. Her choices continue to inspire fine jewellers and high-street designers alike to this day.

A 19-year-old Diana is photographed outside her Earl's Court flat, wearing her trademark pearls and knitwear, 1980.

The power of pearls

In Diana's rollercoaster of a life, there were few constants, but pearls were always close to hand. In some of the earliest paparazzi photos of Diana, captured outside her flat in Earl's Court when she was dating Prince Charles, she can be seen wearing a classic pearl necklace. In the months before her untimely death, she was spotted in Washington, DC, wearing a pearl necklace at an American Red Cross event and a similar necklace to attend the funeral of her friend, fashion designer Gianni Versace.

It's rumoured that fashion phenomenon Coco Chanel once said of pearl necklaces, "Why wear one string when you can wear two?" It seems Diana encountered this notion and decided to take it a few steps further, sporting as many as seven rows of pearls at a time.

Some of Diana's favourite earrings featured pearls, notably the pearl and diamond drop earrings she was given on her wedding day by the Spencer family jeweller, Collingwood. Eagle-eyed fans will know that she wore the same pair both on her wedding day, with her pink "going away" outfit, and with the revenge dress. Make of that what you will.

Princess Diana wears a pearl necklace and earrings on a visit to the American Red Cross in Washington, DC, 1997.

"*I think Diana was probably a bit of a magpie – there's a real* core identity *that comes through her jewellery, because she did a lot of it herself.* She enjoyed it."

AMY ROBERTS

The Princess of Wales proves she isn't one to shy away from statement pieces with this pairing of jumbo pearls and larger-than-life sunglasses, 1989.

One of Diana's favourite and most versatile pieces came in the form of a sapphire brooch, seen here at a banquet at Hampton Court Palace in 1982.

Sapphire: the royal stone

A wedding gift from her grandmother-in-law, The Queen Mother, Diana's sapphire brooch remained a constant feature of her attire throughout her many reinventions. Fashion historian Suzy Menkes explains, "The Queen Mother's wedding present to Diana was a duck egg of a sapphire, surrounded by a double row of diamonds and mounted as a brooch." Diana wore the attention-grabbing item pinned to the lace trim of her oh-so-eighties Bellville Sassoon dress when she attended a Downing Street banquet in 1981. She later wore the brooch at Hampton Court Palace for a state banquet in honour of Beatrix, Queen of the Netherlands, attaching the huge blue jewel to the vibrant tangerine sash of the Order of the Crown.

Ever the rebel, Diana did not keep this dramatic jewel as a brooch for long. She had it reworked as the centrepiece of an on-trend, seven-strand pearl choker, which she wore to concerts, the Met Gala and even to The White House, where she hit the headlines after being photographed dancing with John Travolta. In 1994, the necklace was the finishing touch to her infamous "revenge dress", perhaps worn as a final snook cocked at the family who had abandoned her. The historic piece hasn't been seen in public since 1994 and it's presumed it was inherited by her sons. Having been photographed in The Queen Mother's sapphire earrings and Diana's engagement ring, perhaps Kate will eventually appear wearing the sapphire. Valued today at over £100 million, it is one of the most expensive jewels in the royal collection.

The Cartier Tank

Another piece that accompanied Diana from her late teens to her late thirties was the Cartier Tank watch. Defined by its slim style and square face, the watch came to market in 1919, but the French jeweller wouldn't see success with the model until the 1970s, when celebrities like Andy Warhol and Jackie Onassis began to wear it. During their marriage, Diana often wore a gold edition of the watch that Charles had given her on her 20th birthday, but after their split she appears to have pushed this one to the back of the cupboard, switching for the Cartier Tank Louis, with an alligator strap, which her father had given her. Current fans of the style include Michelle Obama, Angelina Jolie and Meghan Markle.

Diana smiles at photographers on a 1995 trip to Argentina, wearing her Cartier Tank watch and clutching a Dior bag.

Athleisure sweatshirts

Graphic sweats were one of the key fashion pieces of the eighties and nineties. As the younger generation rejected wool jumpers and poplin shirts, the cotton crew neck became a canvas for brands and institutions to play with, making ordinary people and A-listers alike into walking billboards. Luckily for the wearers, the printed sweatshirt was also seriously comfortable.

Diana's approach to the graphic sweatshirt was almost always tactical. Many would look at the sweatshirt as a straightforward item of comfortable clothing, but Diana understood its power. The princess used her sweatshirts as a tool to deter the press, as with the blue Virgin Atlantic sweater she grabbed for nearly every gym session throughout the mid-nineties, or as a way of promoting the causes closest to her heart – as with the white British Lung Foundation top she wore in the early nineties.

Though she was said to have failed her O levels (the equivalent of GCSEs) twice, Diana's sweatshirt game gave the impression that she was an alumna of some of the most elite universities in America. Her cowl-neck Harvard sweatshirt is one of the most recreated numbers, with brands such as H&M and countless Etsy sellers mimicking the look.

"It's an awesome talent, fashion-wise, to take things that look pretty normal and make them look almost unhinged. On most women, it's what we call personal style. On Diana, it reads like a psychologist's notepad," says fashion journalist Rachel Tashjian.

"*I believe as her body became* **fit, strong** *and* **healthy,** she **felt empowered** *and ready to face those bad times head-on.*"

JENNI RIVETT

"Famed for her pastel cycling shorts, oversized collegiate jumpers and Reebok Classics, Diana's downtime wardrobe embodied the 'People's Princess' moniker given to her by the media."*

ALICE NEWBOLD, *VOGUE*

Dressing down with juxtaposition in the form of the Gucci bag. London, 1996.

A love of loafers

Much has been said about women's relationship with shoes. Most quotations on this topic are the type of thing you'd find on a cushion at TK Maxx. But we can agree that shoes are a pretty key way to tell the world who you are. You could probably tell Diana's life story just by talking about her footwear choices over the years, but there was one particular style that would see her through – the loafer. She displayed a marked preference for the shoe throughout her life, from her days of awkwardly trotting through West London as photographers worked to catch a glimpse of the 19-year-old who was rumoured to be dating Prince Charles, right up until her final humanitarian trip to Bosnia in 1997. Diana's love for the loafer would outlast her marriage. The Tod's Gommino driving shoe is usually cited as one of Diana's favourite styles: the former princess was captured wearing the suede shoes in a range of colourways, including classic tan, soft sky blue and light khaki. Other notable fans of the style include Chiara Ferragni and Suki Waterhouse.

These Tod's loafers would become one of Diana's signature styles. She wears them in tan on a 1997 trip to Angola.

In case you missed the loafers, Diana demonstrates her love for Tod's once again with this choice of handbag, 1997. The Italian company named the "Di" model after the Princess of Wales.

Diana's denim

From the mid-eighties, Diana began to wear a wider range of denim styles, from light-wash dungarees to classic Mom jeans. Her preference for denim was not only a fashion statement but also a token of her accessible status as the "People's Princess".

Daniel Miller, a UK anthropologist who has studied the significance of the denim favourite, describes the power of jeans as follows: "Jeans convey the idea of being a simple, unaffected, everyday kind of person, friendly and inoffensive [...] Jeans cause no bother, physically or socially."

With this in mind, we might speculate that Diana's affinity for denim went beyond a style preference and was in fact a signifier of her desire to be "normal" and connect with her peers as she navigated the complex world of royalty, fame, motherhood and her own independence.

Diana's denim looks are often the most beloved of her outfits for her present-day admirers, a generation who have become fans of the late princess on TikTok and Instagram. And what pair of jeans is more timeless than Levi's 501s? Diana wore the denim classic with an oversized tee on school runs or a simple white blouse on philanthropic missions abroad.

"They're simple, they're not complicated," says Lynn Downey, archivist and historian at Levi Strauss & Co., about the original Levi's 501 jean. "It's just denim, thread and rivets." And yes, Diana was bitten by the double-denim bug. She's seen on the following page with a young William and Harry on a ski holiday to Austria in 1993.

"*Don't call me an icon. I'm just a mother trying to help.*"

PRINCESS DIANA

Diana pairs high-waisted indigo jeans with a matching shirt, leather jacket and white snow boots while on a ski trip to Austria, 1993.

The tank dress

The shift dress, the tank dress – whatever you want to call it, it was one of Diana's favourite styles throughout the nineties. It made such an impression that *Vogue* referred to it as Diana's "secret weapon". And one unlikely name stood out from the rest – Versace. Though designers like Jacques Azagury and Catherine Walker dressed Diana in the pared-back style, the Versace tank dresses were the ones that really captivated the press.

Defined by its low-cut, rounded neckline and simple straps, the dress style was worn by the late princess in one of the most extraordinary photo shoots of her lifetime. The November 1997 cover of *Harper's Bazaar*, published two months after her untimely death, shows Diana in an embellished, ice-blue Versace dress (overleaf). The shot was captured a full six years before her death but wasn't featured on the cover until afterwards.

There are two other Versace tank dresses that sit among Diana's best looks: a black, figure-hugging model that featured two button straps, and a white number with silver charms on the straps that she wore in 1995 at the Children of Bosnia charity concert in Modena, Italy. "The sample Versace shift dresses were probably her most successful looks to date," Diana's former stylist Anna Harvey told *Vogue*.

Diana attends a private event at Christie's in a pale blue number by Catherine Walker, 1997.

"The sample Versace shift dresses and evening columns that Catherine Walker was doing for her were probably her most successful looks to date."

ANNA HARVEY

The silk Versace gown that Diana wore on the cover of *Harper's Bazaar* is displayed at a 2017 exhibit entitled *Diana: Her Fashion Story*, hosted by Kensington Palace.

ABOVE Diana wears Versace to an Italian fundraiser event, 1995.

OPPOSITE This Versace tank dress was one of Diana's favourites,
worn here to the *Apollo 13* premiere in 1995.

Pink power

There's never been a more divisive colour than pink. Which made it the perfect hue for a revolutionary figure like Diana. For the better half of the twentieth century, the colour has, for many, signified femininity. In the 1940s, American parents were encouraged to use pink to indicate their baby's sex – and the trend spread from there. It's a complicated colour: some see it as the shade of frivolity or a hue best reserved for the "dumb blonde" trope, but others believe it to be a powerful colour that should be embraced and reclaimed.

In *Pink: The History of a Punk, Pretty and Powerful Color* by Valerie Steele, the fashion historian notes, "Jayna Zweiman and Krista Suh chose the colour pink [for the knitted hats worn by women on feminist protests, beginning in 2016], they said, because it was 'a very female colour representing caring, compassion and love – all qualities that have been derided as weak but are actually STRONG.'"

As Diana navigated royal life, the colour pink communicated her non-threatening, almost angelic character. In the nineties, she reclaimed the hue as a power move. Pink came to represent the unapologetic softness of her character. She described this best herself in her notorious 1995 *Panorama* interview. In response to journalist Martin Bashir's question about why she thought she might not have been accepted by many of the royal family, she stated, "Because I do things differently, because I don't go by a rule book, because I lead from the heart, not the head, and albeit that's got me into trouble in my work, I understand that. But someone's got to go out there and love people and show it."

A hot pink style complements Diana's cheerful demeanour
on an outing in Manchester, 1993.

ABOVE Lady Di wears a pink and white coat dress designed by Catherine Walker and a Philip Somerville hat with a veil to a service at St Paul's Cathedral, 1990.

OPPOSITE Diana pays homage to Jackie O with a tailored two-piece, designed for her by Gianni Versace, on a 1995 trip to Argentina.

Say hello to nineties minimalism at its finest with this straight-cut suiting style in a muted sand colourway, paired with a scoop-neck top, tortoise-shell sunglasses and tan accessories, London 1997.

The blazer

"The item of clothing that makes us feel powerful is the one that makes us feel confident and self-assured, that magically makes us look our best in all kinds of circumstances."
Valerie Steele, fashion historian

We all have pieces in our wardrobes that make us feel powerful. For Diana, the item imbued with this strange magic was probably the blazer. Early on, they appeared in red velvet, then as an oversized addition to nearly every outfit the princess wore. Later, they became her go-to piece to channel a nineties minimalist vibe. The blazer was Diana's preferred pick throughout most of her adult life. It's a garment that demands respect, and which gestured to the world that Diana was not here to mess about – even when it was paired with acid-wash jeans or a midi skirt.

Alice Newbold, the executive fashion news and features editor at *Vogue.co.uk*, wrote in January 2022, "In Diana's hands, the blazer became more than just a signifier of 'business'. She veered from her so-called 'Sloane Ranger' preppy style and paired her jackets with long-line pleated skirts and pumps; tracksuits and cowboy boots. She was seminal in propelling the blazer forward as an all-rounder, not just something to take to work."

It's no wonder that Diana's blazer-based looks are some of her most popular outfits among fashion lovers on TikTok and Instagram. They're just so *her*.

"Blazers were a mainstay of Princess Diana's wardrobe, segueing from the power-shoulder styles of the eighties to chic, continental cuts in the nineties, which were worn with simple chinos or jeans."

THE *TELEGRAPH*

OPPOSITE A red-cheeked Diana dons a red blazer over a black roll-neck during her courtship with Prince Charles, 1980.

OVERLEAF Diana poses in an oversized blazer style for a photo with Harry, William, Charles and Eton headmaster Dr Andrew Gailey on William's first day, 1995.

Collars, collars and more collars

Diana's love of big, bold collars, demonstrated throughout the eighties and early nineties, is impossible to miss. Likely a key influence on the continuing modern-day obsession with the collar (see Ganni and Miu Miu, for starters), Diana's collar collection exhibited some seriously impressive breadth. In her Sloane Ranger years, the Edwardian-inspired pie-crust collar was her go-to style, often worn beneath a knitted cardigan or woolly jumper. She also sported dresses with delicate lacey collars, a look that defined Diana's daintier era.

Pussy-bow blouses featured in some of the princess' strongest eighties looks. Statement collars were just one of the many style elements that showed Diana's dedication to experimenting with the details. A floor-grazing velvet dress in a deep navy blue would be gorgeous on its own – but add a lace collar, and the look becomes a total hit. A teal polka-dot day dress would make the papers by itself, but with the addition of a statement collar, the outfit becomes even more special. Diana demonstrated to the world the power of a big, bold collar – and we're still showing our appreciation today.

Diana dons a feminine frill collar on a
royal visit to Canada in 1983.

OPPOSITE The eighties were all about going bold – and Diana got the memo. Here she's pictured in a polka-dot dress with a bold collar worn on a visit to Auckland, New Zealand, 1983.

RIGHT Diana attends a dinner at the National Film Institute wearing a velvet dress in deep navy with lace cuffs and collar, 1981.

Dior bag

Diana's "cleavage clutches" were named for their role in helping Diana maintain some modesty following a wardrobe near miss during her first official appearance with her then boyfriend, Prince Charles, in 1981. But if we take them out of the equation, Diana's handbag collection was pretty understated. She often opted for the same select styles over the years. Her preference for quality over quantity is evidenced by her two designer favourites – enter the Lady Dior bag and the Gucci Diana bag.

Diana's love of Dior went beyond her favourite handbag. Her glamorous look for the 1996 Met Gala featured a slip dress and silk robe designed by John Galliano during his Dior era. But it would be the quilted Lady Dior bag that would go down in fashion history as one of Diana's most memorable accessories. The bag first appeared on Diana's arm in Paris in 1995, when she attended a retrospective of the artist Paul Cézanne. At the time, the design hadn't yet been released by the French fashion house and internally, it was simply referred to as the "chouchou" bag. The story goes that the bag was a gift to Diana from the First Lady of France at the time, Bernadette Chirac. The exhibition would be the first of many occasions on which Diana would reach for the bag, inspiring Dior to name it the "Lady Dior" in 1996. The design has been reinterpreted in countless styles since, notably for the Dior Lady Art project, which gave artists working across a range of disciplines an opportunity to add their own unique twist to the accessory.

Versace dressed Diana in a bright orange ensemble for a visit to Liverpool, styled here with the iconic Dior handbag. The fashion house continues to sell the bag decades later as a tribute to the late princess.

The Gucci Diana bag remains a favourite with handbag lovers across the globe.

Gucci bag

For Diana's off-duty looks, Gucci's bamboo-handled bag would become a trusted go-to staple. In fact, the design had been around long before Diana was even born. The story goes that Gucci created the bag in 1947 in response to a scarcity of leather in Italy following the Second World War – hence the use of bamboo. Known at that time as the 0633 bag, the model would propel the Italian label to new heights. The unique bamboo feature became a calling card for Gucci's dedication to premium craftsmanship (each handle is lacquered and carefully manipulated into shape by hand).

The 0633 has since been renamed the Gucci Diana bag and adapted for a new generation with a rerelease in 2021. It's a key piece in the "Gucci Beloved" collection, which reimagines Gucci's most iconic bags (the favourite bag of Jackie O, one of Diana's style heroes, was also updated and reissued as one of the series). The 2021 version of the Diana bag features a neon strap and has been spotted on the arms of stars such as Elle Fanning and Jodie Turner-Smith.

Gucci's aesthetic of fusing high fashion with streetwear owes a lot to Diana. Photographs of the princess digging through her 0633 bag, dressed in her signature off-duty look of sweatshirt and shorts, have been shared tens of thousands of times across the social-media platforms Instagram, Pinterest and TikTok. Gucci has cannily capitalized on this free advertising – and on the popularity of all things Diana in this online realm – by rereleasing the 0633 under its new name. It's an It bag for Gen Z, the streetwear-loving generation who haven't known life without social media – the only barrier to its fashion ascent might be its £2,999 starting price.

Her

CHAPTER 4

Legacy

cA new era of appreciation

In the eighties and nineties, Diana fans would have needed to head to the newsstand or switch on the television set to catch a glimpse of the latest statement outfit. These days, Diana's fan base exists in a very different world. Without the distractions of vicious rumours about her love life or her personal struggles, a new generation can admire Diana for her wardrobe and her habit of making a powerful statement via the length of a hemline or the pattern of a jumper.

Her perceived attitude toward the institution of the royal family arguably resonates more with the younger generation today than it did at the time. As our society becomes increasingly self-aware and willing to take a stand against tradition in the name of a fairer world, Diana's talent for rebelling against outdated practices (often through her outfit choices) makes her a welcome role model. This reason for the resurgence of her fame is demonstrated when we consider the most-viewed clips of her on YouTube – her public snooze session during a visit to the Victoria and Albert Museum in 1981 reaching 19 million views by 2023 and her jaw-dropping *Panorama* interview with Martin Bashir, raking in nearly 7.5 million views. These clips record two key moments where Diana, whether on purpose or not, appeared to display a devil-may-care attitude towards "the Firm". Evidently, we love her for it.

Stephanie Yeboah is one of the many online influencers known to recreate Diana's iconic looks, pictured here at the BFI in 2022.

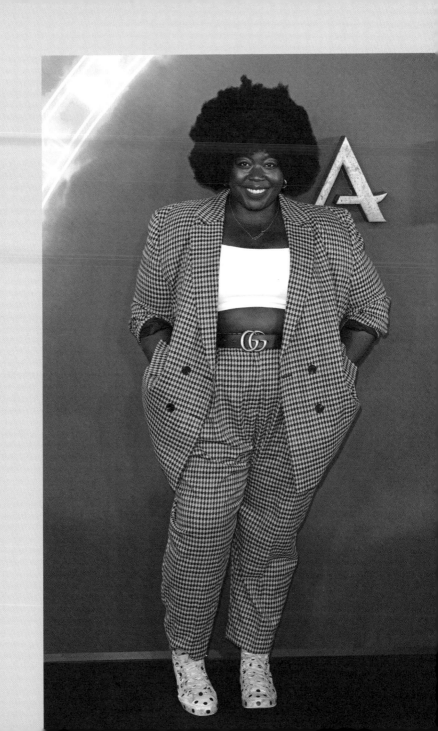

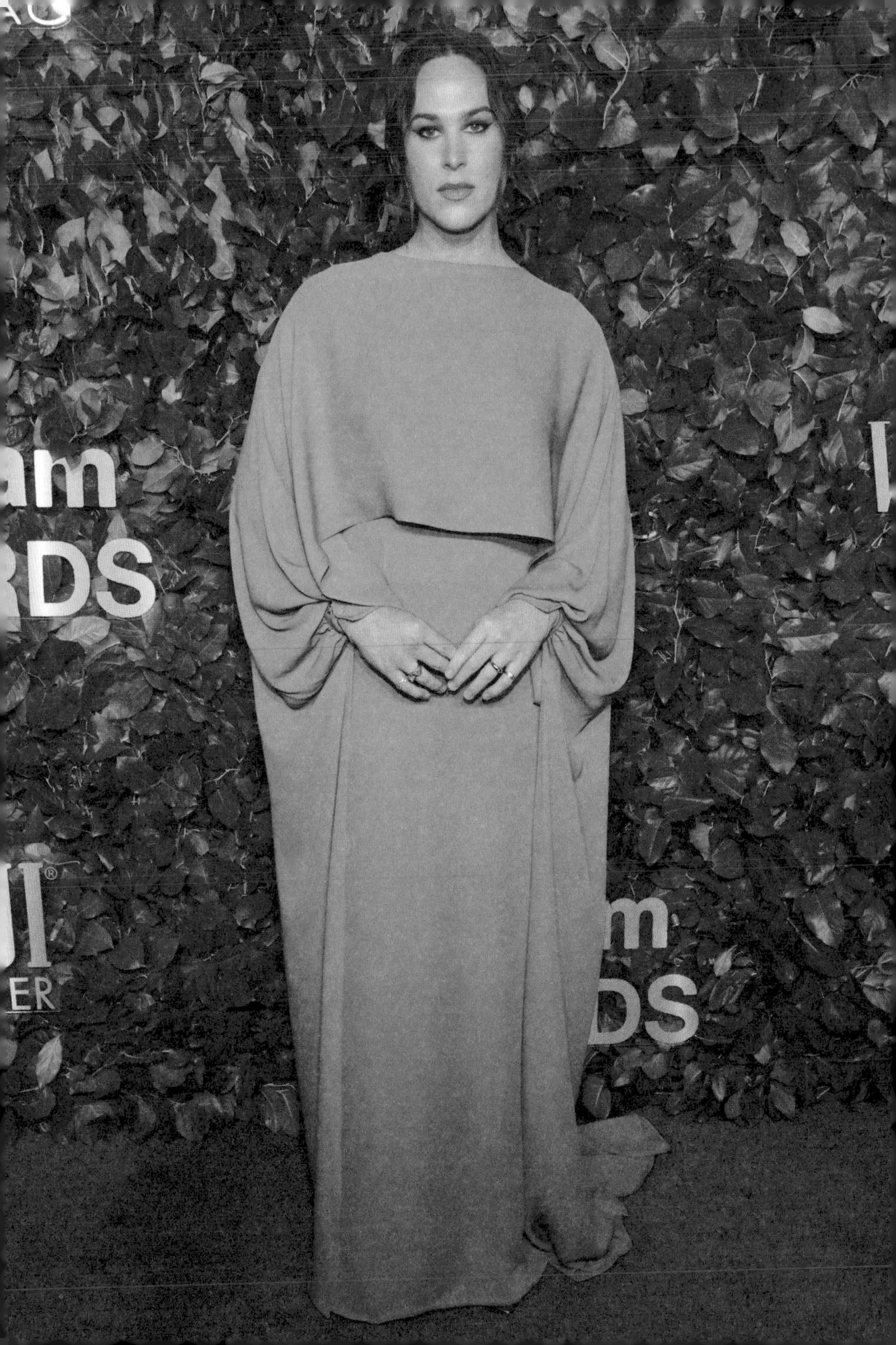

When it comes to Instagram, the number of accounts dedicated to Diana and her style seems to be infinite, and many garner hundreds of thousands of followers. Comments such as "Princess Diana is a different level of woman", "indisputable queen Diana", "How do we dress like Diana – what do we need?" and "a true lady and humanitarian" show how she is remembered by those who were present to witness her life and those who have come to know her after her death.

Diana's reach could be summed up with a checklist of a few of the people emulating her looks on Instagram: a small, representative sample would take in Australian TV personality Liv Phyland, Stephanie Yeboah, an author and body image activist from South London, and American actress and filmmaker Tommy Dorfman.

TikTok has also played a key role in creating a new wave of Diana fans. Countless videos set out to recreate the late princess' most legendary looks, and clue watchers in on where to shop for the necessary components.

Using the handle @simplesmurf on TikTok, Kaden Luna has become one of the most popular Diana fans on the platform. He explained to *Vogue* in 2021 that his obsession with the "People's Princess" began when he saw stars such as Harry Styles and Hailey Bieber reference her in their looks.

Actress Tommy Dorfman showed her respects for Princess Di with her 2021 Halloween ensemble which showed her mimicking the iconic "Sleeping Beauty" look by Bellville Sassoon, posted to her Instagram account and garnering over 150,000 likes.

"The *Diana aesthetic* has endured the ages. Today, brands continue to take cues from *key looks* in the Princess of Wales' wardrobe ..."

THE *INDEPENDENT*

The release of the fourth season of *The Crown* further inspired the Texan influencer. "Me and my #princessdiana sweater collection vs the world", one caption reads. By 2022, his Diana-related content had been watched by hundreds of thousands of people, clearly demonstrating a widespread interest in Diana's fashion legacy.

The *Daily Mail* reported on this surge of enthusiasm for Diana among users of the social media platform, dubbing her "the TikTok princess" in one article from 2021. The piece highlighted a key factor in Diana's popularity with a quote from Gen Z TikToker Jade Honey.

"There's something incredible about a princess wearing the coolest street style, especially back then. A lot of her casual outfits exuded that 'off-duty model' vibe that's so popular with celebrities now. I couldn't imagine the Duchess of Cambridge doing the same thing," the Isle of Wight-based fashion lover told the publication.

American influencer Morgan Riddle went viral in July 2022 when she was spotted in the stands at Wimbledon supporting her pro tennis player boyfriend Taylor Fritz. Her head-turning look was influenced by one of Diana's casual outfits from 1995, as Riddle explained in her TikTok. In just six months, the post was viewed over a million times.

Another post that paid homage to Diana was made in March 2021 by TikTok user Shay Rose (or @crescentshay). It depicted the DIY fashion queen taking an eleven-dollar dress found at her local Goodwill (an American thrifting institution) and transforming it into the iconic "revenge dress". 6.5 million people around the world liked the post.

"*I understand that change is frightening for people, especially if there's nothing* to go to. *It's best to stay where you are. I understand that.*"

PRINCESS DIANA

The head-to-toe look

Eighties make-up and hairstyling was truly something else. Aside from the occasional celeb experimenting on the red carpet, larger-than-life curls and blazing neon make-up represent an approach to beauty that twenty-first-century fashionistas are happy to leave safely in the past. However, while Diana's clothes were typical of her time, her hair and make-up often took a pared-back approach. Dutch TikToker Rose Van Rijn (or @70srose on the platform), proved the timelessness of Diana's beauty regime in May 2021 when she posted a tutorial explaining how to achieve Diana's flouncy hairdo on the social media platform. At the time of writing, the video has been viewed a staggering 20.5 million times. Van Rijn told *Allure*, "Diana is long gone but I hope to carry on her legacy, even if it's just a bit by wearing her hairstyle again and showing it to other people on the internet."

More evidence that Diana's style legacy extends beyond her wardrobe appears in a 2017 video posted by celebrity make-up artist Lisa Eldridge. She remarks that she's been bombarded with requests for her to do a "Princess Diana look". She welcomes a member of Diana's make-up team, Mary Greenwell, to demonstrate how the princess liked her make-up done to an audience of over two million viewers. (Greenwell has now worked with Meghan Markle – interesting to imagine the conversations they must have had.)

Celebrity make-up artist Mary Greenwell is credited for working with both the late Princess Diana and Meghan Markle to help them shine in the spotlight. Here she attends the Fenty Beauty x Harvey Nichols launch in 2017.

(They just get) It girls

I won't claim that Diana was "the original influencer" (though many do), but the popularity of all things "People's Princess" on social media is testament to her long-standing legacy across fashion history and pop culture. And like her, some of Diana's keenest A-list fans inherited their fame through family connections. Celebrity models Hailey Bieber and Kendall Jenner have both publicly demonstrated their interest in Diana's life and style through their attire and in interviews.

Two years after her editorial homage to Diana in *Vogue France*, Bieber told *Harper's Bazaar* in August 2022, "I was really inspired by the fact that she was the most-looked-at woman in the world at that time, of all time, and she did what she wanted with her style. She really expressed herself through her style despite being in the position she was in."

Three decades after the original look was photographed, Kendall Jenner has been spotted in a nearly identical outfit to Diana's ensemble that featured sweatpants tucked into cowboy boots, worn to take Prince William and Prince Harry to school in 1989. Jenner also named Diana as one of her style icons in a July 2019 piece in *Vogue*, noting that Diana's high-waisted, slim-fitting jeans are one of her favourite denim looks.

Hayley Bieber wears an undeniably Diana-inspired outfit while out in Los Angeles in October 2019.

Model Emily Ratajkowski, a close friend of both Bieber and Jenner, has also caught Diana fever, as demonstrated by her enduring love of an oversized blazer and images of her in a pinstripe dress that reminds us a lot of one of Diana's 1996 looks.

"I'm trying to go eighties and have been thinking about Princess Diana's street and ready-to-wear moments like a blazer and a bike short and a big sneaker," she told *Us Weekly* in 2019.

Rihanna has also publicly voiced her appreciation for the Princess of Wales. "You know who is the best who ever did it? Princess Diana. She was like – she killed it. Every look was right. She was gangsta with her clothes. She had these crazy hats. She got oversize jackets. I loved everything she wore!" the pop megastar told *Glamour* in 2013 (it should be noted that Rihanna expressed this sentiment long before the Diana mania that has swept social media in the last few years).

The Barbadian star's appreciation for Diana would only grow over the years. In 2017, she told *W Magazine*, "Whether her choice of this knockdown dress was conscious or not, I am touched by the idea that even Princess Diana could suffer like any ordinary woman. This Diana Bad B*tch moment blew me away."

Kendall Jenner tucks her blue jeans into chunky boots with a boxy blazer while in NYC in November 2019.

ABOVE Diana fan Emily Ratajkowski steps out in New York City wearing
a pinstripe blazer dress similar to one of Diana's favourites, 2018.

OPPOSITE Rihanna wears a Chrome Hearts slip dress, Los Angeles, 2015.

Her sartorial references to the princess include a T-shirt by NYC label Chapel decorated with an image of Diana's face, which she wore in 2016, and a black slip dress and robe from Chrome Hearts, worn in 2015, which looked remarkably similar to Diana's Gucci look at the 1996 Met Gala.

Former boy band frontman and fashion icon of the moment Harry Styles has also mimicked Diana's looks. At the 2020 BRIT Awards, he was seen in a Gucci suit paired with two of Diana's style staples – an oversized collar and a pearl necklace. The stylist behind the look, Harry Lambert, told *Vogue* that Princess Diana was a key source of inspiration. In November 2019, Harry was spotted in a sweater vest from Lanvin that fashion commentators were quick to compare to Diana's 1980s "black sheep" jumper.

The power of Diana's style has undergone exploration by the actors who've played the "People's Princess" in numerous films and TV programmes released over the years. Emma Corrin, the star that depicted Diana in the fourth season of *The Crown*, reworked the "revenge dress" when they attended the premiere of *My Policemen* in September 2022. They starred in the film alongside another of Diana's celebrity fans, Harry Styles. Designed by Italian label Miu Miu, Corrin's captivating, gauzy black number featured an off-the-shoulder cut and dramatically trailing sleeves. The look was finished with diamond drop earrings from Cartier and stilettos nearly identical to those Diana wore on that summer's evening in 1996.

Emma Corrin wears a revenge-dress-inspired look by Miu Miu to a film premiere in 2022.

The star of *Spencer*, a controversial 2021 film based on Diana's life, Kristen Stewart has also been photographed mimicking Diana's looks. The American actress was spotted in November 2021 pairing cycling shorts with a cropped Chanel jacket. A few months later, while attending the Oscars with fiancée Dylan Meyer, Stewart again wore shorts, taking a more tailored approach this time around. Chanel provided an oversized blazer for the outfit, a playful take on traditional menswear. Subverting menswear looks was a favourite pastime for Diana.

Her story: retold

In 2019, Netflix debuted *The Crown*, a series that would present a "semi-fictionalized" version of the history of the royal family. The suspense mounted as fans of the programme (over one million of whom tuned in for the first season) waited to hear when Diana would be portrayed – and by whom. Finally, in April 2019, in anticipation of the programme's fourth season, it was announced that Emma Corrin would be taking on the responsibility of playing Diana: the season spanned the years 1979 to 1990.

Despite the enormous pressure that Corrin experienced while preparing for the role, they told the *Sunday Post* that they had enjoyed the wardrobe and styling: "I loved all the looks. There were three different wigs and I loved them all. I liked the first one a lot because I love younger Diana and her sense of fun."

OVERLEAF Elizabeth Debicki portrays Diana in the fifth season of *The Crown*. Here they look pensive in a bejewelled halterneck dress, 2022.

"She was a young woman very much living her life and growing up in the public eye. She was a concerned mother, a fashionista, there were so many aspects to her that fuelled a media frenzy, a curiosity about her."

ARIANNE CHERNOCK

The costume team on *The Crown*, led by Amy Roberts and Sidonie Roberts, took the task of dressing Corrin as Diana extremely seriously. They even consulted the original designers of Diana's 1981 wedding dress to ensure that the replica was exactly right.

It's also been reported that the team consulted the designer behind the original "revenge dress", Christina Stambolian, before crafting a version for Elizabeth Debicki to wear in season five. The Greek designer was happy to give her approval. "It was important to remember to be very respectful of the original designer," Sidonie Roberts told *Byrdie* in an October 2022 interview. "The revenge dress is such a tricky thing to make – to work out how you even have the opening on a dress like that, how she's going to get into it, you've got a crusted body just draped by delicate chiffon."

It wasn't just the design of the dress that would go on to become so significant – but the term "revenge dress" itself. The world witnessed Diana's moment of rebuke and recovery as comparable to a phoenix rising from the ashes: a fierce power play. Many women appear to have taken note. The most fabulous revenge-dress styles of the years to follow would include Mariah Carey's dramatic 1997 two-piece following the diva's break up with Tommy Mottola (a far cry from her previous wardrobe of sixties-inspired swing dresses) and Bella Hadid's totally transparent Alexander Wang look at the 2017 Met Gala following her split with The Weeknd (Kendall Jenner showed solidarity in a similar see-through style, hers designed by La Perla).

A young Mariah Carey made headlines with her revenge look at the 1997 MTV Video Awards.

Bella Hadid stunned in Alexander Wang with support from best
friend Kendall Jenner in La Perla at the 2017 Met Gala.

Diana on the runway

Numerous designers and fashion houses have noted Diana as one of their key influences season after season. But in 2017 – the 20th anniversary of her untimely death – the whole industry was poised to reflect on Diana's legacy, particularly her enduring impact on the world of fashion. What better way to pay your respects to the "People's Princess" than to dedicate an entire runway collection to her? From Danish indie womenswear label Saks Potts to one of the world's most adored streetwear labels, Off-White, designers raced to pay homage.

Virgil Abloh, the mastermind behind Off-White, declared on Instagram that Diana was a key influence on the label's SS18 collection, three days before the 20th anniversary of her death. The label posted an array of snapshots of Diana, with labels like "mom", "countryside girl", "jogging" and "charity" pinned between the photos, demonstrating the many personas she represented throughout her lifetime. The designs took inspiration from prints, cuts and signature styles that had appeared in Diana's wardrobe and inspired comments such as this one from fashion writer Carrie Goldberg in *Harper's Bazaar*:

"Diana wore white for black tie, daytime and casual weekend activities, but for Off-White's finale, Virgil Abloh decked Naomi Campbell in an amazing ivory evening coat, paired with cycling shorts and a sexy lace-up, perspex-covered heel. This was Princess Di 2.0 at its finest, pairing her activewear with inspiration from her most stately looks and daring accessories."

One of the Diana-inspired looks from the Off-White SS12 RTW collection, featuring a two-piece baby blue skirt suit and stark white sport socks reminiscent of those worn by Lady Di in her gym-going days.

A few months after the collection was presented at Paris Fashion Week, the brand released two limited-edition T-shirts which paid tribute to Diana's wardrobe. The proceeds went towards the American Red Cross and the British Lung Foundation, one of Diana's favourite charitable organisations.

With fans including models Slick Woods and Bella Hadid, and French influencer Adenorah, Saks Potts could teach anyone a thing or two about It girl style. Launched in Copenhagen in 2013, the label has inspired young women across the globe with its rejection of the traditional Scandinavian monochrome aesthetic.

For the label's AW18 collection, designers Barbara Potts and Catherine Saks looked to Diana for inspiration. "[Princess Diana] dared to take chances and dress differently from what you would expect of a woman in her position," the duo told HarveyNichols.com (the present-day web presence of one of Diana's favourite London shopping spots). Potts and Saks also discussed their style hero with Coggles.com. "We would have loved to see Princess Diana wearing the collection we made for her, but we hope she would have liked it."

A few years later, Diana fans were treated to the rerelease of two of the best known pieces of knitwear from the princess' wardrobe – the "black sheep" jumper and a tongue-in-cheek sweater by British knitwear designers Giles & George, with "I'm a luxury" written across the chest and "few can afford" emblazoned on the reverse. New York City-based label Rowing Blazers teamed up with the jumpers' original designers for the new drop, milking its status as a favourite of celebrities like actor Timothée Chalamet and comedian Ziwe Fumudoh to attract the attention of the sartorially inclined across the globe. Comedian Pete Davidson was an unexpected yet fitting choice to model the label's SS21 collection, which included two more iterations of the "black sheep" jumper, in a sky-blue colourway and a zip-up fleece style.

Naomi Campbell wears a double-breasted blazer paired with cycling shorts branded with the Off-White logo for the SS18 collection at Paris Fashion Week.

Forever influential

Drag artist Bimini, whose fashion chops are widely admired by the industry, has been outspoken about taking Diana as their fashion muse. Key tributes have included an outfit worn to perform at Download Festival in 2022 and a Diana-inspired pink look worn for their appearance in the November 2021 documentary *Diana: Queen of Style*. But the RuPaul's *Drag Race UK* finalist's love of Diana goes far deeper, as attested to in an interview with *Kerrang* in July 2022:

"Princess Diana was punk because she went against the monarchy with what she did at the time. Like, listen, she was going to where people had AIDS, during the AIDS epidemic, and hugging someone. Humanizing them was the most punk thing ever – that's the punk attitude."

Fashion writer Justine Picardie articulated her eternal influence perfectly, stating in a 2021 documentary, "Every generation will return to Diana because every generation understands the fabric of life, the fabric of love and loss [...] What we are recognizing is something that reflects in ourselves: in our own joy, our own sorrows, our own grief, our own happiness, our own losses. That's there, in the fabric of her clothes."

Diana's influence continues to span across cultures and generations the world over. And much of this can be attributed to her wardrobe choices. Beyond the daring colourways and striking styles, there was often a message that lay beneath – and communicating through fashion is something that never goes out of style.

Bimini sports Diana's face on a ruched tee while performing at Download Festival in 2022.

Index

Credits

The publishers would like to thank the following sources for their kind permission to reproduce the pictures in this book:

Alamy: BRIAN HARRIS 20; Greg Balfour Evans 22; PA Images 41; Anwar Hussein 52; Francis Specker 55; REUTERS 78; Anwar Hussein 81, 92; PA Images 82; Trinity Mirror/Mirrorpix 127; Trinity Mirror/Mirrorpix 131; PA Images 137; PA Images 148; Trinity Mirror/Mirrorpix 178; Dom Slike 208-209

Getty Images: Tim Graham 9, 10, 14, 28, 35, 36, 39, 44-45, 47, 48, 49, 63, 87, 88, 99, 101, 108, 111, 113, 114, 117, 157, 161, 163, 166, 169, 171, 176-177, 181, 183; Bettman 17, Universal Images Group 18-19; Steve Back 25; Jacob Sutton 26-27; David Levenson 32; Anwar Hussein/WireImage 40; UK Press 56; Princess Diana Archive/Stringer 60, 67, 69, 73, 75, 95, 102, 112, 132-133, 143, 147, 180; Georges De Keerle 70, 72, 100; Central Press/Stringer 77; JUSTIN TALLIS 84-85; Keystone/Stringer 89; David Levenson 91; Pete de Souza 96-97; Julian Parker 118, 119, 120, 125, 126, 167; Tom Wargacki 122; Mirrorpix 128, 129, 170; Anwar Hussein 136, 138, 175; Antony Jones 158; Jack Taylor/Stringer 165; Edward Berthelot 184; Jeff Spicer 189; Mike Coppola 190; David M. Benett 197; BG002/Bauer-Griffin 198; Alessio Botticelli 201; Christopher Polk 203; GEOFF ROBINS 205; Kevin Mazur 211; J. Kempin 212; Karwai Tang 213; Francois Guillot/AFP 215, 216; Joseph Okpako/WireImage 218

Shutterstock: 31, 172; Brendan Beirne 15, 155; Tim Rooke 144; Times Newspapers 151

Splash News: 106-107

Every effort has been made to acknowledge correctly and contact the source and/or copyright holder of each picture and Welbeck Publishing apologises for an unintentional errors or omissions, which will be corrected in future editions of this book.